TANGLED IN THE WEB:
UNDERSTANDING CYBERSEX FROM FANTASY TO ADDICTION

By

Dr. Kimberly S. Young

ISBN: 0-75962-288-4

This book is printed on acid free paper.

Author's Note

Names, ages, places, occupations, and other identifying information have been changed to protect the privacy and confidence of persons who consulted with, or were interviewed by, the author. And some of the cases presented have been factually altered or combined for illustrative purposes.

While this book has been written to assist those who are or may be cybersex addicted, it is not intended to serve as a replacement for professional medical advice. Where appropriate, a healthcare professional should be consulted regarding your situation.

1stBooks - rev. 7/2/01

ACKNOWLEDGEMENTS

While my name appears on the cover, this book is the culmination of many individuals who have helped to make this project a success. First and most important, I wish to thank those who struggled with Cybersexual Addiction and their families for their courage and strength to share their stories in the effort to help others learn the potential of this new addictive disorder. Without you, this book would not be possible. I also wish to thank Kevin Quirk and Art Steinhauer for their time editing earlier drafts of the manuscript and for their thoughtful commentary and analysis. A special thanks goes to my husband, Jim O'Mara, for his never-ending support, love, and encouragement.

DEDICATION

To my sister, Suzie Maras, for all her love and support throughout the years.

TABLE OF CONTENTS

INTRODUCTION

As part of the new era of Internet research, I launched the first study on the nature of Internet addiction in 1994 after a friend whose marriage almost ended because of her husband's obsession with online chat rooms called me asking for help. I soon discovered hundreds of other online users who quickly became hooked on the Internet. Soon thereafter, I published the first book to identify and treat this new addictive disorder: *Caught in the Net: How to Recognize the Signs of Internet Addiction and A Winning Strategy for Recovery*. This pioneer research changed my life forever.

Practically overnight, news of my work became prominent in the national media, with features stories in *The New York Times, The Wall Street Journal, USA TODAY, Newsweek,* and *Time*. My research even appeared in the international press in the United Kingdom and throughout Europe as well as Canada, Scandinavia, and Japan. I was frequently called upon as a media commentator on Internet behavior for radio and television station reports on NPR, the BBC, CNN, Good Morning America, and ABC's World News Tonight. Soon I was receiving weekly cards, letters, emails, and phone calls from people all over the world about their cyber-triggered troubles.

To respond to this emergent mental health concern, I founded the Center for On-Line Addiction, the first treatment center and training institute devoted exclusively to Internet addiction and cyber-related issues. And through my clinical practice, I quickly noticed that an overwhelming number of clients were hooked on adult chat rooms, cyberporn, web cam sex, or sexually explicit newsgroups. These clients confided in me that cybersex was more captivating than watching television, more relaxing than reading a book, and certainly more exciting than playing a good round of golf. For them, cybersex had become a life-changing experience. My clients described how computer-enabled sex created a powerful venue for self-discovery, as they could express their sexual desires in a completely uncensored and uninhibited way when online, often for the first time, which led to a deeper understanding of their own primal instincts.

But once able to explore this alternative side of their sexuality, they struggled with how to integrate these newly awakened sexual feelings into their offline lives. The ability to act out hidden or repressed sexual fantasies made them hunger for cybersex in ways they didn't hunger for real-life sex. They felt preoccupied with going online in search of sexual fulfillment and lied to others about their secret virtual world. Their lives quickly became unmanageable, as they wasted hours online when they should have been working, or they ignored family and friends to spend more time at the computer. Often, they jeopardized relationships and careers and, despite the significant problems their use created, they felt helpless to stop.

Cybersex not only hurt the individual but marriages and families were also impacted. I counseled couples whose once stable relationships were devastated by cybersex, and I met with emergency room physicians and domestic violence counselors about the new cases they were seeing of jealousy and physical assault stemming from online infidelities. I consulted with attorneys about divorce cases prompted by virtual adultery and heard from concerned family members and friends desperate to find help for a cybersex-addicted loved one. I even spoke with panic-stricken parents whose young children experimented with computer sex.

As I travel in professional circles, I hear from therapists working in a variety of treatment settings, ranging from drug and alcohol centers, to hospitals, to college counseling centers, to community agencies who are also seeing similar cybersex-trigger problems in their practices. Many indicated that they wanted to establish specialty treatment programs to address its recovery, but felt unprepared to properly diagnose and treat this new disorder because they knew very little about how the Internet actually works much less about its addictive potential.

Cybersex abuse has even entered the workplace, creating new headaches for companies. Startling new statistics reveal that corporate America has turned into a den-of-sin:

- MSNBC conducted a poll that showed almost one in five people go to cybersex sites while at work.

- Studies show that 70% of adult web sites are hit between the hours of 9-5

- Major companies such as DOW Chemical, XEROX, and *The New York Times* have all fired workers because of pornography in the workplace.

- *USA Today* reported that a major U.S. computer manufacturer installed monitoring software and discovered that a number of employees had visited more then 1,000 sexually oriented sites in less than a month.

- In 1997, the Nielson Media Group conducted a survey that showed employees from the top technology firms, including IBM, Apple Computer Inc., and AT&T have accessed Penthouse thousands of times each month.

- Six employees at an Electronic Data Systems site in Troy, Michigan, were fired for abusing their Internet privileges including one highly regarded systems administrator who, despite several warnings, made 15,000 visits to the same adult Web site in just one month.

Not only does this type of employee Internet abuse reduce corporate productivity, but recently, many ex-workers have launched disability claims under the ADA against their former employers claiming that they suffer from an addiction to cybersex and holding the company liable for access to the "digital drug."

Over the years, more research has been devoted to understanding online sexual behavior and its unique impact on society. Most recently, the journal of *Sexual Addiction and Compulsivity* devoted a special edition to cybersex and the darker side of its psychological influence. New studies and papers on Cybersexual Addiction have been presented at conferences such as the American Psychological Association, the National Council on Sexual Addiction and Compulsivity, and the Employee Assistance Professionals Association. Through my own research and that of others, Cybersexual Addiction has been classified as a subtype of Internet Addiction, as a distinct disorder originating from Internet use.

Today, the Internet has become a way of life that is no longer a minority activity but a rapidly growing, mainstream phenomenon. While news reports and surveys discuss the widespread availability and popularity of online sex, little has been written about how this will influence the sexual behaviors of those who indulge. Will cybersex help or hinder one's sexual attitudes? How will new online sexual fantasies affect subsequent behavior? Will cybersex users come to expect sexual fulfillment in the same variety and immediacy as they can find it online? Will users prefer computer sex to offline sex partners? Is cybersex cheating? What is the seductive lure of cybersex?

Based upon my years of research and clinical practice, *Tangled in the Web* uncovers the brave new world of the Cybersexual Revolution and its influence on our sexual attitudes, thoughts, and offline conduct. As the Internet continues to expand into our daily lives, *Tangled in the Web* offers a critical look at the multifaceted aspects of cybersex fantasy and its potential for addiction and serves as a practical self-help guide for individuals and families.

Cybersex users will gain a better understanding of their own online behavior as I describe the eight motives of cybersex users, shedding light on how computer-enabled sex influences our self-esteem and behavior. *Tangled in the Web* describes who is most at risk to develop Cybersexual Addiction, how the disorder progresses, what drives the compulsive behavior, and offers hope and help for addicts with a comprehensive plan to stay web sober even when relapse is just a mouse click away.

Tangled in the Web also takes a broad look at the impact of Cybersexual Addiction on couples and families. I demonstrate the growing prevalence of virtual adultery and offer ways that couples can rebuild trust and intimacy after a cyberaffair. Family members are most likely the first to spot a cybersex-addicted loved one and often struggle with how to confront this person without anger and defensiveness. I point families in the right direction with a seven-step plan to conduct a "family intervention" and show them how they can support the addict throughout the recovery process. Finally, *Tangled in the Web* provides a compendium of resources including web sites, support groups, treatment centers, and reading materials to help individuals, couples, and families along the recovery journey.

For therapists, marriage counselors, pastors, and related mental health professionals, *Tangled in the Web* will serve as a useful clinical guide to properly assess and treat the disorder and will assist forensic psychologists, law enforcement agents, and the court system in general in better understanding the nature of online sexual deviancy.

I want to note that at times throughout the book, I use the male pronoun he or his when referring to the cybersex user or addict and I only do this for sentence continuity. I don't mean to diminish or deny the impact of Cybersexual Addiction on women who have also struggled painfully with this addiction. I should also note that I am using the term, "Cybersex" to encompass any and all forms of sexual material available on the Internet (e.g., chat rooms, pornographic images, live sex shows broadcast through web cams, downloadable videos, etc.) unless otherwise specified.

Ultimately, I hope that *Tangled in the Web* can help us all see more clearly how cyberspace has made an indelible change on how we live and love. I also offer hope that this book may serve as a meaningful examination on the impact of computer sex for the next millennium.

Dr. Kimberly S. Young

December 23, 2000

CHAPTER 1

THE BRAVE NEW WORLD OF THE CYBERSEXUAL REVOLUTION

"We live in a world where we can get sex delivered to our door faster than a pizza"

Anonymous cybersex user

In the 1960s, the first sexual revolution emerged, as smoking pot, burning bras, and free love became associated with a new open sexuality. The zeitgeist of the times was somewhat hedonistic, especially compared to the conservative Reagan years and the post-AIDs era of the '80s. By the time the early '90s rolled around, the sexual revolution re-emerged, but this time it seemed that the hottest sex in town could be found on a laptop computer.

Underlying the uncensored nature of cyberspace, the birth of a new electronic sexual revolution has been silently taking place. And it is happening in our homes, churches, workplaces, and schools. As we take a close look inside cyberspace, we quickly understand that we now have instantaneous access to almost any type of sexual content imaginable. Pornography that is difficult to buy in our neighborhoods is easily located online within seconds. Interactive chat hangouts let us meet online partners to discuss sexual fantasies and fetishes almost instantaneously. With just a few keystrokes, we can watch someone on the other side of the globe undress live through a web cam.

Sex on the Internet is big business. Unlike any other medium before, we now have a tool that unleashes sexuality in a way that has been traditionally kept at a distance through censorship. And the adult entertainment industry has taken advantage of their First Amendment rights to offer an endless variety of sexual content, with no topic off limits. In addition to commercially owned adult web sites, budding entrepreneurs

1

are able to build amateur adult sites such as Amanda, a single mother of two from Australia. To earn money to support her children, Amanda launched an adult web site where for $9.95 a month, men can watch her perform sexual acts through her web cam. She currently has over 700 subscriptions per month and makes more income than she did in her past job as a waitress.

UNLIMITED SMORGASBORD OF SEXUAL FEASTS

The Cybersexual Revolution is upon us, and online surfers are taking advantage of this unlimited smorgasbord of sexual feasts of cyber-pornography, interactive sex chats, streaming adult video, or live sex shows via web cams. Research by industry analysts estimate that the word "sex" is the number one searched keyword on web browsers and that as many as one third of all Internet users visit an adult web site at least once. For any user, from any computer, online sexual fulfillment is just a mouse click away.

Now let's take a tour of the new cyberspace frontier inside the brave new world of the Cybersexual Revolution to uncover how new sexual technologies, fantasy role-play chat rooms, and the popularization of web cams have transformed our sexual culture and its impact on our daily lives.

Growth of New Sexual Technologies

It seems that whenever a new technology emerges, we find ways to turn ourselves "on." Photography led inevitably to early pornography, cars spawned drive-ins, and the adult movie industry popularized VCRs. Today, we have the Net - originally created for military communications and perpetuated for academic research - used for sexual purposes after its more tame beginnings. At first, users scanned in pornographic pictures from magazines and posted them for others to view. But as the technology became more sophisticated, users realized the possibilities with video clips, 3-D images, and even live video feeds.

Companies like Vivid Entertainment have already created a Cyber Sex Suit with DVD interaction; the suit delivers sensations to various areas of the body at the command of specially adapted Vivid DVD adult movies. Basically, we can see that as the capabilities of the Internet grew, so did the abundance of pornographic images, live online sex shows, and streaming video conveniently downloaded to a user's home or office computer screen. And people can utilize this sexualized technology in privacy so they no longer need to worry about someone catching them walking into an adult bookstore or video section of the local movie seller.

Wired Magazine reports that web-controlled sex toys are also already a reality. Companies like SafeSexPlus have created toys for men and women that respond to patterns of light emitted from a monitor. Other companies are introducing products that produce physical sensations from scratch-and-sniff printouts to force feedback devices that produce tactile feelings just by touching a mouse or joystick. The sexual possibilities of these new devices are endless. Researchers are also experimenting with recording and transmitting physical sensations and emotions. UK researcher Kevin Warwick is at the forefront of such work with "his-and-her silicon chip implants" that he plans to wear along with his wife to test the effects of sending a sensation to another person. Others are working on sophisticated devices that provide tactile feedback and input, hyper-realistic visuals, and audio.

Interactive Fantasy Role Plays

The invention of two-way interactive online features such as email, ICQ ("I see you"), chat rooms, newsgroups, or role-playing games provides a unique vehicle to meet and form social relationships via electronic communication, in a similar fashion as ham radios or Citizen Band radios did in the past. Except in chat, online users are much more anonymous because voice recognition is removed and people are only known to each other by fictitious screen names or made-up handles that masks one's true identity. Such information as gender, race, social class, location, and physical appearance are now cloaked safely behind the computer screen.

On the Internet, online users first meet through typed messages that either appear in a public forum for an entire virtual room to read or as an "instant message" privately sent specifically to a single room member. Users form impressions in their interpretation of a message's tone and

3

content, rather than physical appearance or voice inflection, and create mental images of invisible cyber-pals.

In my last book, *Caught in the Net*, I describe the power of the faceless community and how online users form mental pictures of a chat partner, quite similar to how we form mental images of people we speak with on the telephone whom we have never met before. When you only meet and get to know others through their words on a computer screen, you are free to conjure up your own image of who and what they really are. If he describes himself as good-looking, athletic, and muscular, you might imagine Tom Cruise. If he appears honest and says sweet things, you imagine Tom Hanks. The sounds of his voice, the gaze of his eyes, and the touch of his hand are all supplied by your imagination. Online language has significant power, as words on the screen now have the ability to stir emotional responses. Positive exchanges makes us feel happy, loved, or needed. Negative exchanges make us feel sad, hurt, or angry.

In the case of sexually explicit rooms, provocative language has the power to make us aroused and feel desired. For example, despite living thousands of miles apart, two users, *Sex Machine* from California and *Flower Girl* from Nebraska, created the following sexual imagery:

Sex Machine: We are walking along the beach and the ocean breeze is hitting our faces as I take your hand. I feel the warmth of your body near me, and I can't wait to kiss you.

Flower Girl: My heart beats with anticipation as you suddenly stop and turn towards me in the dusk sky above us.

Sex Machine: I kiss your lips tenderly as my hand rolls up and down your soft, supple body. I feel you tremble with my touch as I gently caress you all over.

Flower Girl: My mouth opens and my lips part to let my tongue slide gingerly into yours, as I reach down and take your hand to place it on my breasts.

Sex Machine: I slowly undo your top and let it slide off your shoulders and I look at your body in the emerging moonlight. "You are beautiful," I whisper as I lean down to kiss your neck and sensually move my fingers over the curve of your back.

Flower Girl: I moan in pleasure and quiver to your touch, as I anticipate making love to you on the beach in the moonlight.

Sex Machine: We lay down and I finally feel the full warmth of your naked chest on mine. We kiss wildly, as my tongue flickers in and out of your sweet lips, and my hand slowly massages your entire body.

Flower Girl: Oh yes, that feels so good as feel your hands gently caress me as we nuzzle together in the soft, warm sand.

Clearly, exchanging sensual dialogue can be an intimate and erotic sexual experience, steamier than reading any *Harlequin* romance novel. Cyber-lovers create whatever fantasies they mutually desire and receive immediate reinforcement from their online partners that intensifies sexual arousal. Most often, highly creative and imaginative people are most likely to indulge and adapt to these role-plays, because they are able to easily visualize the erotic scenario.

To customize fantasies, users select and choose a particular role-play room with themes that cater to almost any erotic desire, such as "Married and Cheating," "Black Man for White Women," "Men for Men," or "Women for Women." The room where cyber-lovers meet implies the type of fantasy they are seeking. For example, in the "SubM4F" room [Submissive Man for Female], participants in the room expect that

5

submissive men are looking for dominant females for sexual role-play. In the "Curious Bi-Men Room," users expect that men curious about bisexuality are looking for other like-minded men for fantasy role-play. To help let others know what they are looking for sexually, users invent specialty screen names, such as "SubM4DomF," or "BiM4M." For example, one woman wanted men to take sexual control of her, so she always went under the handle "Female Sex Slave" whenever she entered a chat room to achieve the desired response from other users.

Given the fantasy nature of these role-play rooms, users also create fake identities or personas when online, often lying about their age, gender, location, or measurements. For example, a fifteen-year-old teenage female from Niagara Falls, New York created the handle "Mr.Right31" and pretended to be a thirty-one-year-old businessman from Silicon Valley. She developed an elaborate story about her online persona.

She explained, "I met dozens of lonely women online who believed anything I told them. I was supposedly single, never married, and a computer engineer who worked at a tech firm in the Valley. To help prove I was for real, I scanned in a picture of an attractive man that I found in GQ magazine. I guess I always wanted to know what life was like as a man, and I could do this in cyberspace. What really gets me is all the women who wanted to meet me offline. They would die knowing I was just a teenager screwing around. Why do I do this? Well, it beats doing my homework for school."

Given the variety of rooms, online users are not limited to just one cyber-fantasy. Users can move from room to room or partner to partner based upon their moods and desires. Cybersex users can even have multiple cybersex encounters simultaneously. That is, multiple "partners" are made available via private message screens that are displayed on the computer screen at once, and the user clicks back and forth from one user screen or sexual scenario to the next. A typical example is Rob, a twenty-five-year-old machinist from Chicago who used the handle "Hot Stud" to chat with four or five women at a time, depending upon which ones kept his interest and described the sexiest scenarios.

Web Cam Sex

Through the popularization of web cams, users can now simultaneously watch an online sex partner undress or masturbate to further intensify the sexual experience. Web cams are small video-like cameras that allow two users to view each other in real time, making it possible for cyber-lovers to broadcast faces or body parts directly through the computer. While watching one another through a web cam, users often use voice chat or talk on the phone to actually hear the other person climax. As one man put it, "Web cam sex is the next best thing to being there, especially with my high speed Internet connection – it's like being part of your own private porno movie." Today, users can use several chat rooms to locate potential web cam sex partners such as "Got Net Meeting" or "Web Cams Only" with a variety of choices that seems endless, as woman explains, "In the first month I had my web cam, I met thirty-six different men. Where else could I meet so many men in such a short amount of time?"

Rebirth of the Child Pornography Industry

With the lack of governmental restrictions in cyberspace, child pornography is more readily available in the United State than it has been since the 1970s. With a click of button, users may transmit, manipulate, and even manufacture child pornography. Child pornography is so abundant and intrusive that an innocent Web search using keywords such as "young" "teen" "child" or "boy" can lead to illegal sexual material involving children. For instance, a friend of mine wanted to learn how to surf the Internet, so I showed him how to navigate the Web on my home computer. We logged online and he typed in my name "Kimberly Young" as a keyword at the Web browser on the screen. My web site came up and a few other related sites followed. But much to our surprise, and to my embarrassment, several adult web sites, including child porn sites, were found, such as "Hot Young Teens Do it All," "Young Teen Pics," and "Young Girls Naked," showing how easy it is to accidentally bump into this material.

Child pornographers can now use the Internet to post collections of pictures for trade or sale, publish trade secrets on how best to meet children in cyberspace, and send *spam* of child pornography pictures to multiple and random online users in hopes of finding others who share their interests. This not only reinforces their beliefs that is it normal to engage in sexual relationships with minors but serves to validate their sexual proclivities, as cyberspace give them a convenient vehicle to meet, interact, and unite with one another.

SEX SELLS

Even if you are not looking for sex on the Internet, the adult entertainment industry has a way of finding you through aggressive marketing tactics to entice new users to try their sites and to increase their hit ratio to boost their advertisement revenue.

Email Advertisements - Each day millions of email users receive unsolicited advertisements for adult web sites with captions, such as "Young Nasty Nymphs" or "Hot Teen Pics," sent complete with a link to the site for instant access. As I lecture to various groups, I typically take a quick poll to see how many people receive these unsolicited adult email advertisements and usually ninety percent of the audience raises their hands. The volume is just incredible.

Page Stealing - The adult entertainment industry cleverly disguises pornographic web sites in hopes of generating new business from accidental searches. *Page Stealing* is the term often used when pornographers knowingly register familiar domain names to launch their web sites that they believe users will accidentally bump into. For example, if you type in the web address *"Whitehouse.com,"* assuming that "dot com" is the correct suffix, a pornographic site will display in the browser, instead of finding the official home page of the White House, which is actually *"Whitehouse.gov."* The developers for the site hope that unsuspecting users will inadvertently reach their site to encourage new business.

Mouse Jacking – Has your computer mouse ever been hijacked? *Mouse jacking* is a new way that the adult entertainment industry traps you into viewing their sites. The major porn providers have implemented newer Hypertext Markup Language code on their pages that does not allow a user to exit the site. New porn pages are loaded when you try to exit the page using your BACK button, making it easy to get stuck in one of these endless porn loops. You must shut down your entire Web browser and start again in order to disable the cycle.

TANGLED IN THE WEB

Not all users start off understanding the possibilities of cybersex. Many "newbies" find that they learn as they go and other users are eager to help teach them how to do this. For example, Marcia is a forty-two-year-old homemaker and mother of five from Montreal. "I was curious what all the fuss was about in these chat rooms, so I started to talk with some people my own age in the Over 40s Chat," she explains. "This is where I first met Michael. We became fast friends, and gradually our conversations progressed to discussions about our sexual fantasies. Chatting with him became such a turn on. He was from Australia, so I rationalized that this wasn't cheating on my husband because there was no possibility we would ever meet in person. Over the months, I became Michael's sex slave and personal play toy. Whatever fantasy he wanted, I agreed to. He wanted to know what I looked like, so I had my son show me how to scan photos into the computer. I lied and said it was to show an online girlfriend. Then Michael told me about web cams. He was dying to watch me masturbate for him. I obeyed and nagged my husband until he bought me a web cam for my birthday. Of course, I lied and told him that my new online friends wanted to see what I looked like, never mentioning Michael. While everyone was away and I was home alone, I sat naked at my computer and scanned down at my body for Michael to watch me. I touched myself as he commanded, and it was the first time in my life that I felt so completely desirable. It was the greatest sexual experience of my life. No one ever made me feel that way before."

Tumbling into Trouble

But as Marcia's story illustrates, the joy of cybersex may come at a big price. While Marcia unleashed her secret sexual desires online with Michael, she didn't realize the damage it caused to her or her loved ones. She lied to her husband and even her son about the web cam and what she

9

really did online. Her habit created harsh arguments with her husband, as he hated how much time she spent at the computer. She neglected her children, as her late-night chats with Michael made her too tired in the morning to wake up, forcing her children to get ready for school by themselves. She stopped driving her children to school events, making her husband drive them. She was so enthralled with Michael that one afternoon, she even forgot to pick her children up after school.

Eventually, Marcia retreated into intense virtual lovemaking sessions with Michael. Michael completely fulfilled her sexual needs, and soon she didn't need her husband's touch. Even though she never actually made love to Michael in the physical world, computer sex with Michael was so incredible that eventually she just felt bored making love with her husband. Inside, she knew that she was hurting her husband, as it would kill him if he found out about Michael, but her feelings for her cyber-lover were so powerful that she could not pull herself away. While she was not in love with Michael, he could please her in ways that no one else could. No matter what the cost, she was determined to protect that relationship.

Marcia is not alone, as many online users who experiment with cybersex often discover it is more enticing and sexually fulfilling than they first imagined. Cybersex offers new dimensions in sexual satisfaction, as the excitement is exclusively driven by fantasy. Computer-enabled sex does not involve physical touching with a partner, but rather sexual satisfaction is achieved through erotic dialogue, visual stimulation, and/or self-stimulation, making it unique from other forms of sexual expression. The seductive lure of cybersex goes beyond anything we have seen before. It offers several advantages that, in most instances, aren't obtainable in the real world. Computer-enabled sex is:

- Unlimited – with hundreds of new adult web sites added each day to millions that already exist, going well beyond the selection found at adult bookstores and porn shops.

- Discreet - giving a curious user the opportunity to anonymously explore bolder and bolder sexual fantasies online without others knowing.

- Diverse – available in a variety of forms such as still photographs, downloadable videos, and live sex shows broadcast through web cams.

- Interactive – a two-way communication medium that allows users to mutually dialogue about intimate sexual fantasies with online partners through chat rooms, newsgroups, and instant messages and lets users arrange real-life meetings for sex.

- Immediately accessible – as web sites are open for business on a twenty-four hour basis, seven-days a week.

- Universal - crossing cultural boundaries that allow individuals to exchange fresh and unique perspectives about sexual behavior that may be considered unusual or bizarre in one's own life.

The Addictive Potential of Cybersex

Computer-enabled sex offers to each user who tries it the ability to act upon any sexual proclivity or fetish imaginable within the safe confines of his or her home or office. With its strong appeal, some users start to feel that they need cybersex more than sex itself, as slowly they begin to lose control over their online habit. For instance, one man's need for cybersex was so severe that he urinated in empty soda bottles to avoid leaving his computer to go to the bathroom.

Compulsive disorders can manifest themselves in many non-chemical means, such as gambling, food, shopping, or high-risk sexual behavior, and the mental health field is just beginning to acknowledge the addictive potential of cybersex to the same extent. While research in the addiction field has not been conclusive, most researchers agree that a combination of neurochemical and behavioral bases explain addictive behavior. Studies support the belief that non-intoxicants are equally as habit-forming as substances. As the online user becomes more addicted to cybersex, he begins to engage in several compulsive behaviors, such as:

- Having trouble managing time at the computer.

11

- Feeling preoccupied with using the Internet to find sexual gratification.

- Neglecting daily responsibilities, proper rest, or a healthy diet just to have cybersex.

- Using cybersex to cope with stress, depression, or loneliness.

- Hiding online interactions from others.

- Feeling guilty and shameful because of cybersex.

- Compulsively masturbating when online.

- Experiencing irritability, panic attacks, or depression when forced to go without cybersex.

In cases of Cybersexual Addiction, the addict's appetite for cybersex grows creating significant problems in his life such as social isolation, family troubles, relationship difficulties, divorce, financial debt, poor work performance, job loss, and even legal troubles. The compulsion can even transfer to sexually compulsive behavior offline, as the user may begin to visit strip clubs, buy adult magazines, rent X-rated videos, or become sexually promiscuous – behaviors that the user was not involved with prior to cybersex.

Cybersexual Addiction has even become a major issue among a number of new child custody battles. Concerned wives fight for full custody because they fear that their former husbands are perverts if they discover a husband's online pornography collection and believe he should not be left alone with the children. Concerned fathers fight for full custody because they worry about that their former wives are so addicted to having cybersex that they are unable to care for the basic welfare of the children.

For example, one former husband describes, "We have three young children that she totally ignores due to her obsession with sex chats. Our children often miss breakfast because she is on the computer or sleeping because she was on it all night. Everyone we know, including her own brothers say she is neglecting the children because of the Internet. She is so involved with hot sex chat online that she doesn't think straight. She hasn't worked since January because of her chatting. She even went so far as to ask a guy she met in the chat rooms to live with her. We are now getting divorced and I am fighting for custody of my three children. We have been to a court appointed psychologist to help determine custody. She never heard of Cybersexual Addiction and she looked at me like I had two heads when I mentioned it."

While it seems like cases like this lack credibility because the disorder is so new, recent child custody decisions have supported addictions to technology. On October 22, 1997, *The Orlando Sentinel* ran a front page headline: *Mother addicted to the Internet loses custody of her kids.*[1] In the a precedent setting case, a Lake County judge said that the mother spent so much time online that she neglected her children because of an addiction to the Internet. During the court hearings, a summary of witnesses testified that after the couple separated, Pam Albridge, had moved the computer into her bedroom and installed a lock on the door. She began to spend most of her time isolated in the bedroom with the computer and locked away from her children. Since the news of this case, attorneys, child psychologists, teachers, and pediatricians across the country are starting to see similar custody cases.

The Denial

Despite these problems, most cybersex abusers deny their addiction. Their denial stems from maladaptive core beliefs, rationalizations, and distorted thinking that support the addiction. For example, a husband who surfs the Net late at night for cyberporn while his wife and children sleep upstairs tells himself that he isn't doing any harm to his family. He tells himself that having cybersex keeps him from going to strip clubs or worse, perhaps running around with prostitutes. What he doesn't realize is the quality time lost with his wife each night he goes online. Nor does he think about the lost opportunities to spend with his children, and he ignores how exhausted he feels during work the next day. Cybersex addicts suffer from a variety of rationalizations that serve to justify the compulsive behavior:

- I am oversexed.

- No one will know.
- It's not really extramarital sex - it's just words on a screen.
- No one else is like me.
- Just one more time won't hurt.
- Everyone else is doing it.
- I need this sexual release in order to function.
- My sex drive is just too powerful.
- I can't get addicted to a machine.
- It's been a long day, and cybersex helps me relax.
- It is just one large credit card bill for adult web site subscriptions. I've spent my money on sillier things.
- I can't understand why my spouse complains about my computer use, we never did much anyway.
- I must be okay using the Net all night – I still do well in school (or work).
- Doing chores is just not as important as staying online longer.
- So I miss a few hours sleep from the Net; that's just wasted time anyway.

These are powerful rationalizes to overcome and generally speaking, the addict must hit that metaphorical "rock bottom" to finally admit the problem. What constitutes "rock bottom" varies, in one case, it means losing a marriage, in another case it means losing a job, and still for another it means getting arrested for wrongdoing over the Internet.

Where do go from here?

While not all cybersex users have tumbled into such serious problems, it is quite clear that it has a much greater impact on life than most would care to admit. If you or a loved one is delving into this new sexual frontier, you need to have your eyes wide open to what's around you and where it might lead you. So in the ensuing chapters, I will show how Internet-enabled sexual fantasies develop and progress and fully explore their impact on our lives. In the next chapter, I reveal how this new Cybersexual Revolution liberates users by affording them sexual opportunities and outlets that once were not available, which will help you better understand the dynamics of your own cybersex behavior.

In Chapter 3, I explore the seductive nature related to cybersex by outlining the symptoms and stages of Cybersexual Addiction. To help you understand the disorder, I'll review how the compulsive behavior momentarily allows the addict to "forget" problems, while ultimately creating a vicious cycle that cybersex abusers find themselves in, as feelings of boredom, loneliness, or stress trigger Internet-enhanced masturbation episodes. In the short term, this may be a useful way to cope with the stress of a hard situation; however, addictive behaviors used to escape or run away from unpleasant situations only end up making the addict's problems worse in the long run. Chapter 3 also provides the Cybersexual Addiction Index (CAI), a 20-item questionnaire to help assess if you or a loved one may be addicted.

Cybersex addicts discover that it is difficult to simply go "cold turkey" from the Internet, given our computer-saturated society, which makes it difficult to completely abstain from the Internet in order to treat the addiction. In Chapter 4, I offer hope and help for cybersex addicts with a comprehensive seven-step plan for recovery that shows you how to:

1. Assess your current Internet use practices.
2. Make measurable changes in your Internet behavior.
3. Address how you will deal with abstinence.
4. Understand the sexual needs that drive the addiction.
5. Develop a proactive plan to deal with high-risk situations.
6. Correct the rationalizations that leads to relapse.
7. Find sponsorship and continued support.

This structured recovery program provides concrete tools that help you relieve shame for the behavior, provide new ways to relate to others, and create a positive self-image.

Today, relationships are now faced with new challenges, as cybersex and its use interferes with typical sex drives and creates arguments and emotional discord with a partner. Each week, jilted partners who lost their relationships because of virtual sex, contact me searching for help and guidance. Many are surprised to learn how seemingly "harmless" cyber-romps result in serious relationship difficulties way beyond what was expected or intended. While I find that some couples are able to use cybersex as foreplay and easily integrate it into their sexual repertoire, for others - mainly middle-aged and older adult couples - cybersex spells infidelity and broken trust. In Chapter 5, I provide insight for couples struggling to work through the betrayal and rage caused by cybersex and offer a step-by-step plan to rebuild trust and rekindle intimacy in their relationships.

Family members are often the first to notice significant personality changes when a loved one gradually retreats more and more into the computer. Those closest to the addict feel alone and search for information on how best to intervene and help. In Chapter 6, we'll talk about the impact of Cybersexual Addiction on the entire family. I offer specific steps that family members and friends can take to confront a loved one in trouble. I also offer ways for families to learn new communication skills that will strengthen relationship boundaries and facilitate successful recovery for the addict.

Because many healthcare professionals are unfamiliar with the Cybersexual Addiction, I receive several requests for specific referrals to local therapists or clinics knowledgeable about the disorder. While this book is designed to help bridge that gap, specialists in the field are still difficult to find. Therefore, Chapter 7 provides additional resources, such as Web sites, reading materials, and recovery organizations, to help you along the way. I also offer tips on how you can start a support group in Cybersexual Addiction recovery in your area.

Now, let's take the next step on this important and timely exploration.

CHAPTER 2

ONLINE SEDUCTIONS: THE EIGHT MOTIVES OF CYBERSEX USERS

"Cybersex was my newfound drug, better than Viagra."

- Ben, a retired navel officer

Through cyberspace, ordinary people are given the unique opportunity to explore new aspects of their sexuality in dynamic and creative ways. One grandmother told me how she rediscovered her sexuality again after years of being widowed. "I thought it was so wonderful to write about my sexual feelings," she says. "I grew up at a time when women didn't say or do such things, so talking about sex with men I met through the computer helped free me to explore parts of myself that I never knew even existed." In this chapter, I discuss the healthy applications of cybersex and how users obtain a richer sense of their own sexuality through provocative online stimulation. The emotional and psychological benefits of cybersexuality are varied and diverse, dependent upon the needs of each individual cyber-user, and I have compiled them all in the Eight Motives of Cybersex Users. As we review each motive, you'll discover how cybersex can provide sexual self-acceptance, expand your sexual repertoire, and help you cope with underlying sexual issues in a non-threatening manner.

MOTIVE ONE: Cybersex is a disease-free way to spice up your sex life.

We live in a world where the spread of sexually transmitted diseases, especially AIDs, is a reality that makes people fearful of physical sexual relationships with strangers. However, on the Internet all that changes as virtual strangers can "shack-up" online through anonymous messages without fear of disease, making cybersex the ultimate in safe sex. Because it's safe, cybersex releases our sexual fears and inhibitions. As one woman explained, "I was a cybersex virgin and awkward and wasn't sure what to say my first time. I quickly learned to be more comfortable with it and now I think it's great to have a guilt-free indulgence. What else can you say that about? Chocolate is fattening. Drugs are illegal. And real-life sex might lead to diseases."

In the post-feminist age, women have taken bolder positions on sexuality and now, with the help of the Internet, have an accessible way to take advantage of their new sexual freedom. I recall being stuck in Newark Airport for nearly seven hours, and when we finally boarded the plane to return home, it was another hour before we got off the tarmac. The woman sitting next to me on the plane started up a conversation, and after some small talk she asked me what I did for a living. As I told her, her eyes lit up. Suddenly, she was telling me about her divorce and how she started to "cyber" with men she met online. "Small world," I thought to myself, as she told me that she had just flown in from Texas to meet one of her online boyfriends. She described how she was never really sexually satisfied with her husband and how enjoyable cybersex was as a means to spice up her sex life. She currently lived in a small, rural town and had a hard time meeting men after the divorce. The Internet changed that as she explained, "I can screen out the weirdos without leaving home and don't have to worry about disease."

Couples also can enjoy the benefits of the Cybersexual Revolution as a new electronic way to have foreplay. Cybersex provides them with fresh ideas on how to approach sex in a way that enhances their lovemaking sessions. Mitch, a twenty-six-year-old account executive with a large investment bank in Manhattan, explains how he and his wife used cybersex as foreplay: "It was difficult for us to talk about sex, especially my wife who isn't comfortable asking for what she wants. I taught her about sex chat and we went online together and met people in the "Swingers" chat room, pretending to be interested in threesomes. Cybersex was the most outgoing I have ever seen my wife about sex. She took charge of the fantasy and sometimes I got an erection watching her chat with this other person. After a little while of this, we went to the bedroom and had the most intense sex of our lives."

MOTIVE TWO: Cybersex intensifies self-stimulation and masturbation

Multi-tasking takes on a new meaning as users often masturbate while trying to work the computer. As users experiment with virtual sex, they quickly learn they have the vast potential to have a new erotic experience each time they log on whether they are searching for new pornographic images, or actively meeting new cyberlovers in an adult chat room. And they use this knowledge to heighten sexual stimulation when they masturbate.

Instead of watching the same adult video over and over again, or looking at the same set of adult magazines for self-stimulation, users surf chat rooms to find new sexually stimulating material to use as part of their masturbatory fantasies. Users are able to customize sexual scenarios, as one woman explains, "If I don't like the guy I am chatting with, I instantly click to find a new partner. If he doesn't pan out, I can find another and another until I meet the one I want." Often, users describe the experience as a "quest" or a "hunt" for the right sexual experience. One man described the experience as follows: "I used to masturbate to *Playboy* before I discovered the Internet. Suddenly, *Playboy* seemed boring and didn't satisfy me like online porno. In cyberspace, I continually look for new, enticing images. I wonder what I will find next before I log online in the morning or when I am driving home from work. For a while, I even tried to use magazines to refrain from cybersex, but it just isn't the same. My climax was over too quick and I missed the hunt of looking for new pictures."

MOTIVE THREE: Cybersex provides instant gratification.

Cybersex is life in the fast lane. While it might take days, weeks, or even months to meet someone at a singles bar, it takes only minutes online. The Internet never sleeps, so at any time, day or night, that you feel "in the mood," sexual fulfillment is just a few keystrokes away and without the complications of awkward good-byes. Erotic chat is a fast-paced environment, where questions that would be considered offensive in face-to-face conversations are perfectly acceptable in cyberspace. Within seconds of a virtual meeting, questions such as, "What are your

19

measurements?" "What are you wearing?" "What is your age?" and "Are you married?" are quite common and are expected by more experienced cybersex users.

For instance, I gave a workshop on Internet addiction recovery in Vermont last year. I recall one brave woman who asked me what cybersex actually was. Everyone chuckled, but I could tell that many in the room had little experience with cybersex firsthand but were too embarrassed to ask. Luckily, I had my laptop and a live Internet connection. I typed in the key words "sex chat" into the Web search engine and hundreds of sites were instantly found. I then clicked into one of the adult chat rooms and entered my handle as "Cute_girl."

Not only was the audience amazed at the variety and abundance of sex chat rooms that were listed on the web search engine, but they couldn't believe the handles of the other people in the chat room. Names such as "Horny Teen for Sex," "KinkyM4F," "BiM4M," and others scrolled up the screen and the conversation in the general chat room was more sexually explicit than anything these workshop attendees had ever heard at a local pick-up bar. After a few seconds, I received a private message from "Ken24" that said, "hi, do you want to chat?" and the following chat took place:

Cute_girl: Sure

Ken24: a/s/l (which translates into asking me for my age, sex, and location)

Cute_girl: "20/F/Vermont."

Ken24: Describe yourself, what are your measurements?

Cute_girl: Tell me about yourself first.

Ken24: Tall, dark hair, muscular, 6 foot, 200 lbs, athletic build, and horny as hell.

Cute_girl: You sound nice.

Ken24: Your turn now, babe. What do you look like and what are you wearing?

Before I could type an answer to Ken24, another person with the handle, "WildBill4Fun" sent me a private message asking if I wanted to "cyber" and immediately described his body to me and indicated that he was naked. And yet another person with the handle "Charlie19" privately messaged me to ask if I wanted a sex slave. The audience sat in sheer amazement as within minutes, I had three potential partners for cybersex. But this is cyberspace, with willing cybersex partners and a plethora of sexual opportunities available on a continuous twenty-four hour basis.

MOTIVE FOUR: Cybersex allows you to escape mental stress and tension.

It takes a great deal of time and energy to cultivate a satisfying cybersex experience, and users often find themselves in a "Vulcan Mind-Meld" as they enter an erotic trance-like state.

Many users explain how anxiety-reducing the online sexual experience is. Users are not passively watching the screen, they are active participants in the experience, whether searching for the "perfect" online image or the best erotic chat fantasy role-play. The user's mind is fully absorbed in the interactive and immediate capabilities of cybersex that provides soothing relief from the mental tension of life.

In what I call the "Authorship Phenomenon," cybersex allows us to become authors of our own sexual fantasy experience as each user is given the opportunity to be the author of his or her own, personal illicit novel. While reading erotica is a simple turn-on, interactive virtual sex lets you be the star of your own co-written play. With that power, users become so engrossed in the creation of their online fantasies that they are able to mentally escape from moments of extreme stress and tension.

For example, Nancy, a fifty-two-year-old nurse from Vancouver, discovered cybersex five months ago. She routinely went to the hot sex chat room and met different men for causal cybersex. While Nancy found it all fun at first, she eventually became bored with the same routine, so she decided to try out different types of chat rooms to add some excitement. She entered a room, "DomF4SubM" [Dominant Female for Submissive Male] and played the role of a twenty-three-year old dominatrix. "By day, I am caring and competent nurse, and by night, I train a new batch of cyber-slaves," she explains. "Having cybersex is a highly creative and intellectually stimulating process. My mind is so completely focused on developing the fantasy that I forget all my roles and responsibilities in life, for me, cybersex is the ultimate escape."

MOTIVE FIVE: Cybersex normalizes your sexual fantasies.

Sex is such an important part of being human, but for most, sex is rarely discussed openly. Our families said very little, if anything, about sex around the nightly dinner table. For the most part, we learned about sex from friends, books, or high school health class before our parents even thought to talk with us about it. And if our parents did talk about sex with us, they often sent implicit messages that "masturbation is bad" or "wait until you are married before having sex." I recall my own father teaching me about sex by going to the public library and making me read books that outlined the biological process of sex. While I had a thorough education in reproduction, I didn't learn much about the emotional impact of sex in my life.

Cybersex changes all that. Instead of sex being hidden in adult bookstores located in the outskirts of town, cyberspace provides us with an opportunity to enhance our own self-understanding with messages of virtual acceptance. The cyberspace culture also provides a safe forum to be honest about one's sexual thoughts which helps the cybersex user normalize his sexual feelings.

Carol is a forty-three-year-old woman raised in a strict, Southern Baptist family. In her marriage of twenty years, she considered sex beyond the missionary position to be dirty, and her inhibitions created sexual tension and problems in her marriage. She discovered cybersex after a friend of her invited her to the "hot tub" social chat room, where she met "Latino Lover" online and was able to open up for the first time about her sexuality. "At first, I had a difficult time even typing sexy on the computer, given my repressed upbringing. But through this relationship, I was able to connect to feelings I was too embarrassed to admit that I had and my Latino Lover made me feel good about myself," she recalls. "Actually, the whole chat experience drew me closer to my husband as I was more open to experiment with sex afterwards."

MOTIVE SIX: Cybersex provides approval and affirmation, especially for the disenfranchised.

We all feel a little insecure about our physical appearance. Some of us worry about hair loss, the wrinkles that are starting to show, or that our tummies have widened too much. Mistakenly, people make judgments about their own bodies by comparing their figures to those depicted in movies, magazines, and commercials, often those with perfect physiques, making us feel even more insecure about our own body shape. At some point in life, we all fear that we don't have the ideal figure. Yet, cybersex can change all that, and actually provide approval and affirmation about our weight, figure, or receding hairline.

Gail is a forty-six-year-old administrative assistant from New York who always felt uncomfortable with being thirty pounds overweight. That is, until she started to engage in web cam sex. "At first, I preferred hot sex chat because I could hide my body from my online partners," Gail explains. "One partner in particular insisted I buy a web cam, so we could see each other. He lived in France so it wasn't like we could easily meet each other for sex. I was initially apprehensive, but I thought I would try it, so I broke down and bought a web cam. My God, it was the best thing I did. My web cam lover brought me to new sexual heights, as I panned down my naked body while at the computer and I could see how excited he got from looking at me. He made me feel so good to be naked and I actually forgot about all my body insecurities. Instead, I felt sexy, desired, and even a little kinky."

Cybersex also provides productive benefits for traditionally disenfranchised populations, such as the disfigured, the disabled, gay and lesbian populations, and bisexuals. Adam writes, "I am twenty-two from Oslo, Norway, with Asperger's Syndrome, a subset of autism that effects social development among other things. I've spent between four and fifteen hours a day online for the last four years now and currently maintain an online relationship with a woman from Austin, Texas. I have had cybersex with more people than I can conveniently count, while physically in real-life I am a virgin. Having never had a girlfriend before, I feel like a genuine social reject. Because of my disease, women generally don't want anything to do with me. If it wasn't for cybersex, I

23

would have no one. If it were not for my current online girlfriend, I would be completely alone. Women in offline situations in my experience are often complete snobs. I try and approach them and am quickly told to get lost. They also seem to find me extremely threatening, when quite often all I am trying to do is make friends with them."

As we see, this medium is especially helpful for disenfranchised populations who can utilize cyberspace to meet potential friends and partners. Many live in rural areas without access to support groups or establishments, or they are painfully shy because of their situation. The Internet serves a useful purpose in helping them reach out beyond their community. As one gay male explained, "I had little luck meeting men offline, but I discovered so many wonderful resources and meeting places online. The Internet allowed me to virtually screen out potential partners without fear of catching AIDs, which is the best form of safe sex that I know of today."

While we have made much progress with tolerance, self-acceptance of one's homosexuality is still complicated by coping with a homophobic society. I have seen friends as well as clients become depressed and suicidal because it was difficult to come to terms with their sexuality. Sometimes a strong religious background or family upbringing has made this self-acceptance more difficult to work through. Therefore, the Internet helps people who have been afraid to admit their homosexuality, or who fear rejection by others, to freely explore their feelings in a safe online environment, thereby gaining the much needed support missing in their lives in order to start to cope with their feelings. As one woman explained, "I struggled with my sexuality for years. I lead a homosexual life online while maintaining an outward heterosexual life offline. While many think this might be sick, I think it is the only way for me to deal with it until I can come to terms with my inner demons."

MOTIVE SEVEN: Cybersex alleviates performance anxiety.

Performance anxiety may cause "situational" sexual dysfunction, such as premature ejaculation, impotency, or vaginismus (muscle spasms in women that can make sex painful), which are extremely traumatic and hinder normal intimate relationships. Cybersex won't help these conditions that are attributed to medical conditions, but often for mild cases, in which psychological anxiety and panic surround the sexual act, it will help to improve self-confidence and overcome these underlying insecurities. Ultimately, we are all sexual beings, yet many of people feel awkward about their lovemaking skills and feel like they don't know what they are doing in bed. Because no one is physically evaluating the quality of your sexual performance, cybersex helps to build personal confidence through the affirmation generated by online partners who can provide soothing reassurance that we are vibrant lovers.

George, a twenty-eight-year-old software engineer from Boston, describes how cybersex helped him to overcome his performance anxiety. "I didn't have much experience before I got married and then I was divorced two years later," he explains. "Sex with my ex-wife was mechanical and very dull. Internally, I didn't see myself as a very good lover, so I felt intimidated dating. When I discovered adult chat rooms, it changed my life. All of a sudden, women found me sexy. I masturbated nightly with online babes who otherwise might not pay much attention to me had I met them at a bar. But online, I developed a persona that got their attention and appealed to their every whim. There was nothing off limits – bondage, threesomes, urination, – whatever floated their boat, I instantly satisfied them. I was an online *Casanova*. Many were so grateful, they even sent cards and gifts."

Carol had always led an active sex life until becoming menopausal, when she started to experience a loss of vaginal lubrication that made sex painful. She explains how cybersex helped her to deal with her performance anxiety and lead a more fulfilling sex life: "My change of life had such a negative impact on my self-esteem, and I gradually became frigid around men. What started out as a normal part of aging grew to be a deep-rooted psychological problem for me. I became nervous and worried excessively about sexual intimacy, expecting pain all the time. Emotionally, my life was spiraling downward until I discovered cybersex. The ability to go online and talk about sex with men in adult chat helped me to let go of these inhibitions, and slowly my attitude changed. All the anxiety that shrouded sex disappeared behind the screen, which gave me renewed confidence and reduced my tension about making love. I even met my current boyfriend online and he and now share a wonderful relationship, full of trust and passion."

25

Cybersex can also benefit couples who have struggled with sexual intimacy in their relationship because of performance anxiety and its related emotional and physical issues. Ben was a retired navel officer who had suffered from periods of impotence over the past few years. Married for thirty-five years, he and his wife had practically stopped having sex because of his fear of failure each time they tried. For Ben, the discovery of cybersex helped him to build new confidence and cope with his impotency. "Cybersex was my newfound drug, better than Viagra," he explains. "Making love to online women, and being good at it, helped me to learn how to sustain my erection. I realized that a larger part of my impotence problem was a lack of confidence, and over the past few months, I have initiated sex with my wife and it was successful. I can't begin to say how much cybersex has helped me."

MOTIVE EIGHT: Cybersex helps you cope with the pain of childhood sexual abuse.

Sexually abused children often develop into adults who are fearful and distrustful of sexual experiences. As children, sex was a traumatic and shameful experience. As adults, they cope by mentally disappearing during sex, associating sex with something dirty, and/or disowning their sexual feelings because of that experience. In many respects, cybersex provides a corrective emotional experience, as survivors of abuse often report that they feel mentally present during cybersex, associate sex with something positive, and take ownership for their sexual desires when online. For example, Karen is a forty-eight-year-old paralegal at a law firm who describes how her earlier childhood abuse influenced her cybersex experiences:

"My childhood sexual abuse began when I was eleven. I had a very domineering, alcoholic father and up to that point had suffered much verbal and physical abuse from him and had witnessed a lot from him to my mother. When I reached puberty, he became somewhat nicer to me, and this is when the sexual abuse began. I was trapped in this situation, and my mother didn't know about it. It continued for several years on into my high school age and (I found out later) was also happening with a younger sister.

I married the first man who showed an interest in me. My husband is a dear man, and we have gone through a lot in our twenty-eight years of marriage. I kept my abuse to myself for years. I am not sure what started the conversation, but I finally revealed my abuse to him after ten years of marriage. He was very understanding about it. Later, my mother found out through him, and I felt awful. If it were my choice she would've never known, because my Dad had died a few years earlier and I didn't think it right that it should come out at that time. My mother at first scoffed at it and called me a liar, the very scenario that I feared. Thankfully, my younger sister came forward and confirmed that it indeed had happened to her and that was that.

About this time, I lost all interest in sex with my husband and discovered masturbation. I had never had an orgasm until one day when I masturbated. I don't know why, but I feel I love my husband, but sex with him was not very good. I tried to talk with him once, but he just didn't seem to get what I needed. While we are best friends, over the years as the kids grew, we rarely had intercourse. As of today, it has been three years since we last had sex.

When I started chatting on the computer, my life changed. I learned about men's (and women's) sex lives through intimate conversations. It is extremely interesting to me to learn about other people's lives and the sexual aspect was especially thrilling. I have had literally hundreds of sexual conversations with men, and they aroused me to the point of reaching orgasm later with this fantasy "picture." Cybersex became very empowering to me. I know that sounds strange, but for the first time, I feel like I enjoy sex when I talk with men on the computer. My secret online fantasy life has been a healing experience. Through the Internet, I no longer have that "out of body" experience that I had all my life. For the first time, I feel sexually connected, less afraid, and I love every minute of it."

As the case of Karen illustrates, victims of childhood sexual abuse are able to work through the inner pain carried with them for years since their abuse through cybersex. Many times, adults abused as children want help but don't know where to begin and cyberspace provides a comfortable starting point. However, I want to make it very clear that the healing power of cybersex is tricky, and cybersex should not be considered a panacea to "cure" cases of childhood sexual abuse. It happens that adult

27

survivors are also at risk of being revictimized through the reenactment of the abuse while online, and they continue to reinforce painful past events that can strengthen destructive notions about their own sexuality. Therefore, if you are an adult survivor of childhood sexual abuse, it is important to proceed carefully and even seek out professional guidance before trying cybersex so you will minimize the risk of revictimization.

As we look into the future, we can see the many potential positive effects that cybersexuality can have to help individuals develop healthy sexual self-esteem and behaviors. Overall, cybersex helps to clarify and correct misinformation about sexuality and normalizes our sexual interests, which is especially beneficial for minority and disenfranchised populations. Cybersex is also helpful for persons who struggle with issues they are not yet ready to acknowledge offline, such as sexual orientation or being a survivor of sexual assault, but who might tremendously benefit from "lurking" for a while and seeing how others deal with similar issues. In the next chapter, we'll turn our attention to the addictive nature of cybersex and show that despite cybersex's many benefits, it is also too easy to get caught in the web.

CHAPTER 3

WHEN CYBERSEX BECOMES AN OBSESSION

"A moment comes for every addict when the consequences are so great or the pain is so bad that the addict admits life is out of control because of his or her sexual behavior."

Out of the Shadows
by Patrick Carnes, Ph.D.

John is a forty-three-year-old engineer living in Maine who considered himself a devote Christian and good family man. In his life, he had never purchased an adult magazine or rented an X-rated video. He loved his wife of seventeen years and considered her his best friend. He routinely played basketball with his two teenaged sons, attended their school games, and always enjoyed spending quiet evenings at home with his family.

Things among the family were stable until they bought a new computer equipped with AOL for the boys' education and for John to update the household finances. One night, he clicked on "People Connection," which brought him into a lobby of a chat room. He scanned the variety of available member chats, and saw themes such as "Hot Tub" "Cybersex" and "SubM4DomF." Out of curiosity, John clicked into the "Hot Tub" chat room to watch the action, only to be amazed at the open, frank, and blunt sexual content being discussed among chat room members. One woman privately messaged John, "You horny? Wanna chat with a buxom blonde?" "I am new here, not sure what you mean," he responded. The woman replied, "I love a new cyber-virgin to teach." John typed, "I am married." She typed, "That's okay, anything goes here. I just want to make you feel good all over. It's harmless fun, I promise." "How do we start?" John curiously asked, and with that message, he had his first cybersex session with a California blonde.

29

Soon, John was spending nearly four hours a day cybering with various women in the sex chat rooms. He graduated from the "Hot Tub" chat to the "MarriedM4F" chat rooms. His handle also changed from "John43" to "Hard Man." John discovered a secret world as he had cybersex with women from Texas, Germany, Ireland, Canada, and New York. Each taught him new things about sex. They talked about having sex in wild positions, using sex toys and vibrators, and having sex in public places as others watched. Things John would never consider doing in real life, especially with his wife, but all seemed so erotic and tantalizing online. The cybersex progressed to phone sex with these women, whom he often called using phone cards he bought without his wife's knowledge.

As John's online world grew, his real life began to suffer. He stayed up late to chat, only to wake up fatigued for work the next day. He lied to his wife about what he did online, often telling her he was doing the household bills. John suddenly withdrew from his entire family. He hardly played basketball with his sons and never attended school events. He made excuses about needing to do work, while in reality, he stayed home alone to have cybersex.

His use became so excessive that the family bought a second phone line just for John's Internet habit. John never let his son's use the computer, which caused several arguments at home. He completely ignored his family, and soon, his wife demanded that John pay more attention to the family. John denied that anything was wrong, and insisted he needed the computer for work and household finances. Before, he rarely argued with his wife and now, each night, they argued about his retreat into the den. One night, his wife even discovered a phone calling card and wanted an explanation. He said it was for work, but his wife was growing increasingly suspicious about what he *really* was doing online. John tried to rationalize that this was all just fantasy; meanwhile, he saw that this was hurting his family and feared that his wife would discover his secret online life.

To avoid the trouble brewing at home, he began to use his computer at the office for cybersex. He came in early and stayed late. Sometimes, he even telephoned the women for phone sex from his office phone. Some women emailed him naked photographs of themselves, and a few told him about adult pornography sites that he might enjoy. John surfed some of these sites when the cybersex seemed dull, or he couldn't find a willing partner right away. He had amassed 800 pornographic pictures over a span of three months, including pictures of traditional sex, bondage, group sex, bestiality, and even some child pornography. He kept them stored on disks but forgot to delete them from his computer hard drive at work.

John's work productivity suffered dramatically because of his online activities. He knew he needed to go cold turkey from cybersex, but felt the stress of his life overwhelming. Each day, he promised himself that today would be the day he would quit. He was disciplined enough to delete all the bookmarks to the sex sites and bury himself into work projects. A week or two of "good behavior" was always followed with internal dialogue that tempted him to return to cybersex. He rationalized to himself: "I need to relax," "Just a few minutes of looking won't hurt," or "No one will know." Finally, he would break down, enter his favorite chat spots, and a few minutes escalated into hours. Soon he was back to his old daily Internet habit.

John, a once-valued employee, was now missing deadlines and meetings, and his boss suspected there was a problem. His employer began to monitor John's computer account at work to look for incidences of Internet abuse.

The FBI started to conduct its own investigation into John's Internet activities after an agent spotted his handle trading child pornography in an adult chat room. Over the next two months, agents had enough evidence to arrest John for trafficking in illegal pornography. When the FBI seized his computer, they found hundreds of pornographic photographs and at least fifteen depicted children. John cried as they took him away in handcuffs. He lost his job and his wife eventually filed for a divorce.

THE EMERGENCE OF A NEW DISORDER

John's case is an example of Cybersexual Addiction, a disorder that is specific to cyberspace. He had been a faithful and attentive husband. He wasn't the type of man to rent adult videos, or buy Penthouse, or call a 900-phone sex line. He had never visited a prostitute or gone to a massage parlor. He had no prior criminal history or signs of inappropriate sexual behavior in his past.

John's entire sexual world revolved around the computer and the events that took place in cyberspace. Behavior that began for John as a harmless curiosity developed into a daily habit that he no longer could control. The discovery of adult chat rooms and online pornography transformed his computer from a practical business tool to a unique and secret sexual stimulant. John showed all the basic symptoms of addiction: a preoccupation with the Internet, lying about the behavior, a loss of interest in other people only to prefer more time online, using the Internet as a form of escape, and an inability to control his behavior.

With the widespread availability of the Internet and its accessibility to sexual content online, we have seen the growth of a new disorder that affects those who previously did *not* experience sex in an addictive manner. My clinical studies show that nearly *65% of all cases of cybersex abuse happen to people with no prior history of sexual addiction.*[1] A recent survey conducted by Jennifer Schneider similarly showed that only 30.9% subjects report that cybersex activities were a continuation of other compulsive sexual behaviors, such as phone sex, voyeurism, seeing prostitutes, and going to massage parlors.[2] Most commonly seen was a heavy involvement with pornography (magazines, videos, movies, etc.), often since the teen years. Each year new cases of Cybersexual Addiction are reported, as cyberspace becomes a convenient vehicle for sexual exploration and experimentation. Recent studies suggest that approximately 200,000 people already suffer from this disorder, but warn that this may be an underestimate.[3]

Unlike sexual addiction, Cybersexual Addiction originates through actions that begin *inside* the computer, and has more to do with fantasy than the actual sex act. Let's take a closer look at the characteristics of sexual addiction and how this behavior differs from Cybersexual Addiction. Acts of sexual addiction may involve offline events such as:

Random Heterosexual Relationships

Prostitution

Exhibitionism

Voyeurism

Indecent Liberties

Child Molestation

Incest

Rape

In contrast, acts of Cybersexual Addiction typically involve:

Chatting about sexual fantasies

Self-stimulation and masturbation

Real-time viewing of each other's bodies using web cams

Watching live sex shows broadcast online

Viewing online pornographic images

Viewing streaming video

Phone sex with people met through the Internet

Subscriptions to adult newsgroups

Clinicians have argued that Cybersexual Addiction is a subtype of Internet addiction, with its origins in cyberspace usage. Even among activities that are not confined to cyberspace, such as phone sex or real-life meetings, a potential partner is first selected through an online meeting. Rather than turning to strangers through the 900-phone sex lines, the cybersex addict first establishes a relationship via the Internet and screens out possible candidates for phone sex. Or, instead of meeting prostitutes, a relationship is initially cultivated online before deciding to meet for real-life sex.

The computer becomes the center of the cybersex addict's life. The addict's interest in cybersexual activities surpasses all other interests and the behavior escalates until life progressively becomes unmanageable and the extent of the addiction is increasingly apparent. Some examples are:

33

- The user experiences panic attacks and anxiety when he can't log online.

- The user alienates himself from healthy sexual relationships away from the computer.

- The user becomes depressed because of the addictive behavior.

- The user risks getting AIDs by having sex with strangers met over the Internet.

- The user lies to a partner about what he does online all night.

- The user loses sexual interest in a partner because of cybersex.

- The user becomes socially isolated and hurts friendships because of cybersex.

- The user stops taking care of his children just to surf for adult web sites.

- The user secretly uses his office computer for cybersex, unbeknownst to him; his employer is monitoring the Internet account.

- The user moves from cybersex to phone sex and lies about the telephone bill to a partner.

- The user progresses from pornographic online images to web cam sex.

- The user misses work or is less productive because he surfs adult web sites when he should be working.

- The user's son or daughter discovers the online pornography hidden on his computer.

- The user is arrested for trafficking in illegal online pornography.

- The user's spouse leaves him because of his latest cyberaffair.

- The user boss's discovers pornography on his work computer and he gets fired.

- The user attempts to curb his cybersex use and starts to buy pornography, rent adult movies, and/or visit strip clubs.

WHO IS MOST AT RISK?

Cybersexual Addiction spans across age, gender, race, and culture – basically anyone with a computer and modem is vulnerable. However, highly creative individuals with active imaginations or those who suffer from low self-esteem, body image dysfunction, childhood sexual abuse, depression, anxiety, obsessive-compulsive disorder or who grew up in a highly religious family or have a family history of addiction, are at greatest risk. Cybersex addicts may also suffer occupational problems such as job burnout or unemployment and social problems such as divorce or the recent death of a loved one, and use cybersex to distract themselves from their unpleasant situations. One consistent factor among cybersex addicts is that they tend to suffer from poor impulse control and often have a history of multiple addictions to alcohol, tobacco, drugs, gambling, food, or sex.

Clearly, if an online user already suffers from a history of sexual addiction, cybersex serves as another outlet for gratification that feeds a previous problem. The mix of online sexual material combined with a history of sexual addiction leads to a recursive cycle as each activity reinforces the other. For example, Jason is a forty-year-old truck driver from Canada who writes: "My sex drug of choice is masturbation. I am a world-class masturbator and could win a gold medal, if there was one. My drive for sex contributed to my divorce. I had affairs, saw prostitutes, and spent time making obscene phone calls, which came to an immediate halt with the advent of *69! After the divorce, I built up a large credit card debt, mainly by pursuing sexcapades like prostitutes and phone sex talk. I gave up prostitutes long ago (after getting beaten up), and I had to declare bankruptcy, due to my costly addiction to telephone sex chat. Some time before my bankruptcy I heard about Sex and Love Addicts Anonymous. I read books, attended meetings for a few months, and even abstained from masturbating for a record seven days until I discovered a hot sex chat room and masturbated my little heart out. I need to act out sexually when I am alone. It makes me forget about the rest of my problems, I guess. I feel like dirt and then I masturbate those feelings away and I can go on another day. Sometimes this situation seems so complex that I feel hopeless that it can be unraveled and a truly healthy life achieved. I know I need help! I don't want to live the last half of my life alone, whacking off in front of the computer or on the telephone. I get depressed, which keeps the cycle going, with no exit in sight."

WHAT DRIVES THE ADDICTION?

Fantasy is the drug of cybersex. As I described in Chapter 1, adult web sites and role-play chat rooms are available on demand that cater to any sexual desire or need imaginable, from straight to gay, from bondage to bestiality, and from fetishes to incest. For the addict, the fantasy theme begins and progresses as a novelty created through cyberspace. If a woman is curious about what it would be like to make love with another woman, she can enter the Lesbian Sex Chat room. If a black man is curious about what it would be like to have sex with a white woman, he can enter the Black Man for White Woman chat room. If a man has a foot fetish, he can enter the Foot Fetish room to find others who share his interest. If a woman wonders what it would be like to be with an older man, she can enter the Older Men for Younger Women chat room.

Computer-enabled fantasies are highly reinforcing and the addict's preoccupation with sexual arousal stems from his own imagination and fantasy history. The association of the Internet with sexual arousal is so potent that it transforms the Internet from a practical business or research device into a modern day sex toy. As one man explains, "I get a major erection just by clicking on my computer." Sometimes, just recalling the potent images of one's last cybersex episode triggers arousal and reinforces the notion that cyberspace is an open gateway for immediate sexual fulfillment.

The variety and scope of these computer-enabled fantasies are limitless and still evolving. In the post-Internet era, new chat rooms, new technology, and new online users all help to build new sexual fantasy experiences. Individuals who are unhappy and frustrated with their current sex lives are more likely to become addicted to the endless possibilities that computer-enabled fantasies provide in order to satisfy unmet or hidden sexual needs and desires.

For instance, Barbara is a fifty-one-year-old teacher and grandmother who got involved with sadomasochistic chat rooms. Raised Mormon in rural Utah, she had never been able to express or act upon her desire to be controlled by men. She led a conservative lifestyle and conformed to her church teachings, except when she went online. "My whole world changed when I discovered the Internet," she explains. "Since high school, I always wanted to be completely dominated by a man, but I hide my desires because I feared that I would lose the respect of men I dated. They were always good Mormon boys, including my husband who would simply die if he knew I liked this type of thing. For the first time in my life, I can act upon fantasies kept bottled up inside of me. Now, I go online and pretend to be a young girl and watch as my "masters" stand up for me and fight *over me*. When I meet with my masters, I fall naturally into my slave girl persona. The fantasy is so real that I literally cry out in painful pleasure while at the computer. The problem is that I am now obsessed with my submissive girl persona. I can't even make love with my husband unless I think about my masters. This is really starting to hurt our marriage."

As I also described in Chapter 1, behind the anonymity of cyberspace, online users can conceal their age, marital status, gender, race, vocation, education, or appearance. A teenager can say he is an adult, a short brunette can say she is a tall blonde, an overweight man can say he is thin, a married man can say he is single, and a janitor can say that he is a doctor. Cybersex addicts are sexually more adventuresome and prefer to use their anonymity to seek out greater sexual thrills by taking on fictional personas or character roles when online to embellish the fantasy.

Raymond is a fifty-eight-year-old successful executive in a Fortune 500 company, who immersed himself into a new and exciting cyber-fantasy persona. "Actually I am just a horny old man with an imagination that is way too wild for the lifestyle I lead," he explains. "To unwind in the evenings, I use the screen name "Hung Stud" and act out fantasies with women who are actually my own age in real life, but online believe I am really a twenty-year-old college student who loves older chicks. I've gone as far as to post on my profile a picture of young, muscular, and handsome man that I cut out of a magazine to add to my believability. I guess the experience makes me feel young again."

In order to deal with the double-life that occurs, the addict often rationalizes the behavior and disowns what he says or does online with self-statements as, "It's just a computer fantasy" or "This isn't who I really am." Cybersex addicts detach from the online sexual experience and perceive their secret fantasy world as a parallel life that is completely separate from whom they are in real life. However, these rationalizations are temporary and eventually break down as the addict becomes more and more disgusted by his online actions and experiences episodes of despair, as promises to stop are broken and attempts to quit fail.

In many respects, it is easy to understand the allure of cybersex when you can be anyone, say anything, and no one else will know. The make-believe online sexual adventure is independent of reality, as it doesn't matter if a cyber-lover is really telling the truth or just pretending, the sexual satisfaction and intensity are just the same until something happens to break the spell. For instance, Charles is a forty-eight-year-old software engineer in London who discovered hot sex chat rooms. He entered into one entitled, "OldrM4yngF" [Older man for younger female]. Very quickly, he met users with handles like, "young&sweet" "tenderlips" and "Angel4U" who acted like young and sexually hungry women who told him how much they desired him and would do anything he asked. Charles commented, "For less than twenty bucks a month, I get the best sex of my life over the Internet," as he chatted and masturbated nightly with these women, that is, until he discovered one young woman was really a man in disguise.

SEXUALLY DEVIANT ONLINE FANTASIES

Given that the cybersex addict lacks proper impulse control, he is more likely to dabble in sexually inappropriate or deviant material, which is easily accessible through the Internet. This is especially troublesome when the cybersex addict experiments in pedophilic and incest theme chat rooms with names like "Daddy for Daughter," "Barely Legal Females Wanted," and "Horny Teens for Sex," which abound in cyberspace. While these are branded as "fantasy only" chat rooms, it is difficult to decipher what is fact and what is fantasy, based upon the chat dialogues. For instance, when one curious woman entered the "Hot Incest" fantasy role play room, she was immediately propositioned by another user, "So what is your pleasure? Do you want me to be your dad, brother, son, or uncle?" Therefore, it is unclear from the discussion if users are describing fictional stories, sexual fantasies, stories about past activities, or plans for the future.

The risk of experimenting in sexually deviant online fantasies is that the addict begins to distort what normal sex is. "I masturbate nightly to nasty and kinky online pornography," explains one husband, "What turns me on the most is the "devious" aspects of viewing otherwise inaccessible photos, such as naked teens, water sports, and scat pictures. Now, sex with my wife seems so dull in comparison. When I do have sex with my wife, I am always fantasizing about the pictures I recently saw from the Web. This is destroying my marriage. We are now sleeping in separate bedrooms and I am alone all night with my computer instead of her. I know this is sick. I want to quit doing this and restore our relationship, but I just feel too weak to stop."

Cybersex addicts who dabble in sexually deviant fantasies online also risk arrest and incarceration. Recently, I worked with a thirty-four-year-old minister arrested for possession of child pornography he obtained from the Internet. He had suffered from a long history of alcoholism, clinical depression, and extreme problems managing money and debt. He explains his developing interest and the inability to control his inappropriate urges once tapped into. "I soon discovered the vast array of pornography, including child pornography, available on the Internet. My attraction to pornography on the computer was borne of sheer amazement at the volume of available material. And this amazement turned to fascination, and ultimately to obsession. I knew it was wrong to look at this material. My life became a lonely isolated mess. I realized that I could loose my job, my marriage, and the respect of everyone I love if I was caught. I have two daughters and would never think about doing anything inappropriate with them, but I could not bring myself to stop despite knowing all the consequences for my actions."

Unlike classic child sex offenders who exhibit chronic and persistent patterns of sexualized behavior toward children that typically begin in early adolescence, many recent arrests for cyber-pedophilia involve first time offenders with no previous history of sexual activity towards children[4]. Many of the subjects were in college, some still in high school. The compulsivity associated with their behavior was revealed upon interview as many admitted to the long hours they sat in front of their computers collecting child pornography, some with over 40,000 image files collected. Often, there was an obsessive quality to their collecting, as these image files were divided and subdivided many times into folders according to age, hair color, sex acts portrayed and many other categories. The amount of time it takes to download one picture, view it and place it in a file folder, multiplied by the size of the collection demonstrates the large investment of time these behaviors represent.

Clearly, I am not suggesting that all first time virtual sex offenders suffer from Cybersexual Addiction. However, given the clinical profile among many new cases, forensic psychologists, law enforcement agents, and the court system in general have begun to question the role of Internet-enabled pathology in the development of inappropriate and deviant online sexual experimentation, especially as it relates to pedophilic interests. For instance, in a precedent setting legal case, Kenneth McBroom, a New Jersey lawyer, had been arrested by the FBI for possession of child pornography that he obtained from the Internet. His attorney argued that he suffered from an addiction rather than attributing the behavior to pedophilia. Based upon a very complex clinical history, including sexual addiction, alcoholism, drug use, overeating, marital problems, and a history of sexual child abuse, the court determined that Mr. McBroom suffered from a mental condition that significantly reduced his capacity for choice and his online actions were attributable to a compulsion.[5]

THE FIVE STAGES OF CYBERSEXUAL ADDICTION

Rita is an accountant for a large manufacturing firm in Texas. She has been married for ten years and has a seven-year-old son. She describes her descent into addiction: "The anonymity and accessibility of the Internet allowed me to sexually experiment. This experimentation has been good in the sense that I found that other people on the Net had similar interests, and it has helped me accept and love myself as I am. But

I also realized that pursuing these desires would destroy my marriage and my family life. I do this uncontrollably at the office, and it is already hurting my career. This is why I came to the conclusion that I had to face these urges. There was a time when I thought I could mix both the exploration of my desires and preserve what I love of my business and family life. But I quickly came to the practical realization that, just like an alcoholic cannot drink one drink without risking going on a binge, I cannot risk one visit to a sexually explicit site without going on a binge and not being able to stop."

As the case of Rita shows, the habit-forming nature of cybersex is very powerful. Cybersexual Addiction is a progressive problem. It rarely gets better. Over time, it gets more frequent, more extreme, or both. At times, when the addiction seems under control, the cybersex addict is merely engaging in one of the common traits of the addiction process in which he switches from sexual release to the control of it. The control phase inevitably breaks down, whether it is for an hour, a week, a month, or a year, and the addict is back in the behavior again despite his promise to himself or others never to do it again. When the ecstasy of the release is spent, the addict will often feel remorse at his failure and, with great resolve, will switch back to another "white knuckle" period of abstaining from the behavior until his resolve weakens again.

Without help, this is the way the cybersex addict lives his or her life. Even though the majority of the problem occurs within the context of a virtual online world, the disorder impacts one's ability to function in the offline world and the user escalates deeper into the addiction until life becomes completely unmanageable. Ultimately, cybersex addicts are a hidden group. The activity is done alone, in isolation, making addicts feel they are the only one going through the craziness of the problem. They can't understand why they fall into certain habits about the types of chat rooms they visit, or the adult newsgroups they subscribe to, or the nature of the porn sites they visit. And they feel helpless to stop.

The Cybersexual Addiction process cycles through five successive and interdependent stages. The progression through the stages and the change from use to abuse may be gradual or it may occur suddenly, even within days or hours after discovering cybersex.

41

1. *Discovery* – For many users, the discovery that this type of material is openly available in cyberspace is the first stage of addiction. In the discovery stage, a man doing research online may accidentally bump into a pornographic web site or a woman enters a social chat room and meets a man who entices her to have cybersex with him. In either case, the person discovers the sexual thrill of the act, which opens the door for further sexual experimentation to occur.

2. *Experimentation* - Encouraged by the anonymity of electronic transactions, an online user will secretly begin to explore sexual material online without the fear of being caught. In the experimentation stage, a user may try out different chat rooms and sites to see which are the most exciting. Eventually, the user develops a proclivity for a particular room, or set of rooms, or types of porn sites that provide the best erotic stimulation. In this stage, users believe that they can control their urges and deal on their own terms with their virtual experience.

3. *Habituation* – With repeated exposure – like building a tolerance to alcohol – a user gradually needs more and more of the Net to achieve satisfaction. In the Habituation Stage, the online user becomes bored with routine fantasies and now looks for the next big virtual thrill. A user may download more obscene and lewd online pornography, gradually escalate to web cam sex, engage in bolder and more explicit chat fantasies, or may use more graphic online handles such that "Jonboy" changes to "10 inches for You," or "Pamela" changes to "Cyberslut." As the user becomes desensitized to online sex through the constant saturation of sexual themes that take on riskier and riskier forms, the user requires more sexual intensity to achieve the desired effect.

4. *Compulsivity* – The habit develops into a compulsive obsession. In this stage, life becomes unmanageable, as relationships or careers are jeopardized because of the compulsive behavior. In his pioneer

book, *Out of the Shadows*, Patrick Carnes best explains sexual compulsivity:

The sexual experience is the source of nurturing, focus of energy, and origin of excitement. The experience turns into a relief from pain and anxiety, the reward for success, and a way to avoid addressing other emotional issues in the person's life. The addiction is truly an altered state of consciousness in which 'normal' sexual behavior pales by comparison in terms of the excitement and relief from troubles that is associated with sex.[6]

In the same way, the cybersex addict's online sexual experience produces an altered state of consciousness that becomes associated with tension reduction and the addict displays a progressive retreat into use of the computer as a means to avoid life's complications and responsibilities. In this stage, the cybersex addict's compulsive behavior is largely driven by increasingly painful states of tension and agitation, as an alcoholic is driven to drink at moments of excessive stress or an overeater is driven to binge on food during moments of tension. The cybersex addict exhibits addictive patterns as he becomes preoccupied with the computer, attempts to conceal the nature of his online activities, and continues to engage in the activity despite its known potential risks. The more stressful life becomes, the more the addict depends upon cybersex as an escape. At this point, cybersex no longer seems to be a voluntary act, but an involuntary act that must be completed.

5. *Hopelessness* – In this stage, the addict hits that metaphorical "rock bottom" only to realize the extent of damage done because of his or her addiction. Feelings of hopelessness and helplessness develop, especially as the addict becomes fully aware how out of control life has become because of cybersex. The addict realizes the unhealthy excess of the behavior only to attempt total abstinence. Addicts will cancel their Internet service, disconnect

43

the modem, or install filtering software in the attempt to stop the compulsive behavior. The addict struggles with staying clean and sober and feels desperate to put his life back on track. Since relapse is only a mouse click away, he may relapse back into old patterns, beginning the cycle once again. In the hopeless stage, the addict starts to engage in negative thinking about himself, making such self-statements as:

I am helpless because I can't control my use.

I am weak.

I am unlovable.

I am defective.

I am worthless or disgusting because of my 'dirty' habit.

Everything I do is wrong.

I am a failure.

I am trapped.

I don't have the willpower to stop using.

People despise me for my addiction.

My family has given up on me.

There are so many demands on me, I can not handle them all.

I don't have anything else to look forward to, so I might as well keep using.

I don't deserve anything better in life.

My future is empty and meaningless.

Things can only get worse.

The addict feels overwhelmed through these errors in thinking in such a way that he exaggerates the difficulties of abstaining from cybersex and minimizes the possibility of corrective action. At this point, he feels as if his craving to use is stronger than his willpower to stop.

THE CYBERSEXUAL ADDICTION INDEX (CAI)

Has cybersex added to your life or has it become an unhealthy habit? How can you tell if you have crossed the line? It is such a new disorder that many people aren't really sure how to diagnose the problem or how to measure its impact on real life. The following self-examination will help you assess your addiction and impairment levels in terms of mild, modcrate, and severe. Based upon the five-point scale, select the response that best represents the frequency of behavior described in the following 20-item questionnaire.

0 = Not Applicable

1 = Rarely

2 = Occasionally

3 = Frequently

4 = Often

5 = Always

1. How often do you neglect other responsibilities to spend more time having cybersex?

    0   1   2   3   4   5

2. How often do you prefer cybersex to sexual intimacy with your partner?

    0   1   2   3   4   5

3. How often do you spend significant amounts of time in chat rooms and private messaging with the sole purpose of finding cybersex?

    0   1   2   3   4   5

4. How often do others in your life complain about the amount of time you spend online?

        0   1   2   3   4   5

5. How often does your job performance or productivity suffer because of cybersex activities at work?

        0   1   2   3   4   5

6. How often do you become defensive or secretive when anyone asks you what you do online?

        0   1   2   3   4   5

7. How often do you become anxious, nervous, or upset when you are unable to access sexually oriented web sites?

        0   1   2   3   4   5

8. How often do you fear that life without cybersex would be boring, empty, and joyless?

        0   1   2   3   4   5

9. How often do you masturbate during cybersex?

        0   1   2   3   4   5

10. How often do you snap, yell, or act annoyed if someone bothers you while you are online?

        0   1   2   3   4   5

11. How often do you lose sleep due to late night log-ins having cybersex?

    0   1   2   3   4   5

12. How often do you feel preoccupied with cybersex when offline and/or fantasize about having cybersex?

    0   1   2   3   4   5

13. How often do you bookmark or subscribe to sexually oriented web sites?

    0   1   2   3   4   5

14. How often do you use cybersex as a reward for accomplishing something (e.g., stressful day, end of a task)?

    0   1   2   3   4   5

15. How often do you use anonymous communication to engage in sexual fantasies not typically carried out in real-life?

    0   1   2   3   4   5

16. How often do you anticipate your next online session with the expectation that you will find sexual arousal or gratification?

    0   1   2   3   4   5

17. How often do you hide your online sexual interactions from your significant other?

    0   1   2   3   4   5

18. How often do you move from cybersex to phone sex (or even real-life meetings)?

          0   1   2   3   4   5

19. How often do you feel guilty or shameful after cybersex?

          0   1   2   3   4   5

20. How often do you engage in deceptive or deviant online sexual behavior?

          0   1   2   3   4   5

After all the questions have been answered, add the numbers for each response to obtain a final score. The higher the score, the greater the level of addiction and creation of problems resulting from such Internet usage. The severity impairment index is as follows:

NONE: 0 – 30 points

MILD: 31- 49 points

MODERATE: 50 -79 points

SEVERE: 80 - 100 points

After you have identified the category that fits your total score, look back at those questions for which you scored a 4 or 5. Did you realize this was a significant problem for you? For example, if you answered 4 (often) to Question #8, regarding feeling that life would be empty and boring without cybersex, did you realize how dependent upon it you have become? Does 'normal' sex pale in comparison to the excitement of cybersex? Do you feel that you need cybersex just to become sexually aroused? Does it scare you to even consider giving up cybersex?

Say you answered 5 (always) to Question #11 about the changes in your sleeping pattern. Did you realize how much time you lost due to late-night cyber-romps? Were you aware of just how often you do this? Have you ever stopped to think about how hard it has become to drag yourself out of bed every morning? Have you noticed how this lost sleep has begun to take its toll on your body and your overall health?

In the following chapters, I will outline how Cybersexual Addiction impacts relationships, family stability, and job functioning and I will provide specific techniques for recovery. If you scored over 80 on the test, you are in particular need of this information. If you found yourself in the gray area, with a score of 50-79, I'll help you begin to zero in on the areas of greatest concern to you. Together, we'll construct a new program to a better way of living, both online and offline. And if you scored in the lower ranges, indicating that you only occasionally spend too much time with the Internet, you'll learn simple time management techniques to help you regain control over the clock. As Cybersexual Addiction impacts both the individual and the family, the ground we cover along the way will be equally as useful to partners and friends of cybersex addicts.

CHAPTER 4

THE ROAD TO RECOVERY: SEVEN STEPS FOR TREATING CYBERSEXUAL ADDICTION

"Great men are they who see the spiritual is stronger than any material force, that thoughts rule the world."

Ralph Waldo Emerson

Craig is a fifty-three-year-old network administrator from Cincinnati who became addicted to adult chat rooms and online pornography. He explains the powerful lure that almost cost him his job and marriage: "I chat on office time. Typically, I make up false names or genders for myself, pretending to be other people by sending out pictures and saying they're me, all this accompanied by masturbation whenever I'm alone in the office usually after hours. I waste hours looking for cybersex, finding the right cyberlover, and the right fantasy for the moment. It's like I need to make the experience last as long as I can before I climax. Typing used to be great, but recently I have moved on to phone sex. It's like an extra benefit, making the sex part real and part fantasy. I do a lot of work-related research on the web, but there's almost always one window open on an adult sex site. Some are "pay" but most are free. I have a habit of saving pictures I like, which often leads to megabytes, or GIGABYTES of wasted office drive space that I end up deleting all at once after a while.

This is obviously interfering with my work, and I fear getting caught by my boss. I'm starting to "work" late just for time alone with the computer, wasting money on pay sites. I try to restrict myself from masturbating at home (I'm married), but I will be right back on the sex sites once my wife is in the shower or asleep. The real scary part for me is that I like cybersex better than having sex with my wife. Real sex just doesn't seem as good as it is on the Net, and I know this is starting to impact my marriage. I need to deal with my problem and learn how to back off from this. I find my behavior hard to control, especially because I have constant access to the Net at work.

I TRY to do things to control my urges, such as moving the computer so that the screen is more visible to others, but then I end up blocking the view somehow. I try to put all of my wife's and my email in the same program so that she will see the letters I'm getting, but then I got a hotmail account to be anonymous. I delete all my bookmarks, then spend twice as long finding all the websites again. The longest I have been able to abstain is for up to six weeks at a time. I have thought about trying to use those parental filtering programs on my computer at work to help me kick the habit, but I know my boss would notice if I suddenly put that on the computer. Please help me find a way to stop this craziness."

WHEN THE COMPUTER IS A CONSTANT TEMPTATION

As Craig discovered, our computerized society makes it difficult to simply go "cold turkey" from cybersex. Today, many need to use the computer every day, making sobriety from cybersex more complex. As more and more jobs involve computers and as more and more homes have computers, complete abstinence from the Internet may be impossible, forcing the cybersex addict to use self-control to achieve corrective action and abstinence from cybersex while at the computer. But how can addicts learn that kind of willpower and self-discipline, when any contact with the computer feels like a constant temptation?

RECOVERY WHEN RELAPSE IS A MOUSE CLICK AWAY

Recovery from Cybersexual Addiction is most akin to recovery from food addiction. Food addicts can not simply abstain from food as part of their recovery, instead they must discover healthier ways to live with food in their lives. Similarly, cybersex addicts must discover healthier ways to live with the Internet in their lives. To make this discovery, the addict must readily identify and understand the underlying emotional, cognitive, or situational factors that trigger the addictive behavior, such as depression, anxiety, loneliness, stress, marital troubles, divorce, or career problems, and learn to cope with those underlying issues in a more adaptive manner.

In general, the recovery process is an ongoing self-exploration that must separate the behavior from the person, relieve shame about the behavior, correct maladaptive behavior, and promote opportunities to learn from mistakes. The recovery process must also build relationships, provide new ways to relate to others, and allow for amends to be made. Finally, the process should provide continuous support and affirmation that creates a positive self-image. To reach these recovery goals, I have developed a comprehensive seven-step recovery program designed to help addicts achieve and maintain cybersex sobriety:

1. Assess your current Internet use practices.

2. Make measurable changes in your Internet behavior.

3. Address how you will deal with abstinence.

4. Understand the sexual needs that drive the addiction.

5. Develop a proactive plan to deal with high-risk situations.

6. Correct the rationalizations that lead to relapse.

7. Find sponsorship and continued support.

Using Craig as an example, I will outline how to apply each of these steps.

1. Assess Your Current Internet Use Practices

Having a specific, goal-oriented plan that modifies computer behavior for healthy cyber-use is necessary in the early stage of recovery. To best implement an effective modification plan, it is important to first assess your current use of the Internet. A thorough assessment will help you examine the volume of cybersex use in your daily life and identify high-risk situations, feelings, or events that trigger the behavior. For instance, you may be anxious about a big meeting or you are upset after the boss criticizes your work, so you turn to cybersex as way to deal with these work-related tensions. After a big fight with your spouse, you turn to cybersex to work off your frustration and anger. To help you see how this process works in your life, I have provided an **Internet Usability Assessment Form** for you to fill out each time you log online.

Date and Time	Event	Online Activity	Duration	Outcome

Indicate the day and time of each Net session, the antecedent events leading up to logging online, and the type of online activity accessed (email, chat, pornography sites, stock quotes, eBay, random web surfing). Next, keep track of how long you spend online and mark the number of minutes or hours spent per Internet session. Finally, describe the outcome of the Internet session in terms of what actions were completed, what activities were interrupted while online, or how you felt after the Net session. For example, Craig's Internet Usability Assessment Form for a single day looked like this:

Date and Time	Event	Online Activity	Duration	Outcome
10/25 9am	Had Coffee	Checked Email	35 minutes	Answered email
10/25 12:15pm	Lunch break, market was down	Email, checked stocks and financial information	1.5 hours	Answered email, Went over lunch break
10/25 4:30pm	Caught up on some work	Email, Porn Sex	2.5 hours	No new email or

4:30pm	some work, didn't feel like starting new project, I had a little time to kill	Porn, Sex Chat		email, so wasted time when I should have been working, late for dinner and lied to wife about why I was late
10/25 10pm	Everyone asleep, bored at home	Porn	2.1 hours	Didn't get enough sleep, guilt for doing this to my wife

Maintain this log for at least one week, or preferably two weeks, so that you can obtain a full picture of your online usage. Once you have completed your form for a period of time, thoroughly review your responses to the following questions and determine if any patterns emerge:

1. What time of day do you usually log online?
2. How long do you stay on during a typical session?
3. What do you usually use the computer for?
4. What types of feelings or situations precede cybersex use?
5. What applications are most problematic for you and why?
6. How do you feel after you log off the computer?
7. Does a quick check of your email inevitably lead to cybersex?
8. Do certain emotions or situations trigger your online use?

This usability assessment will help you throughout the recovery process in three important ways. First, it will serve as a journal of present activities so that you gain a baseline understanding of your daily and weekly online activities and how they relate to using the computer for cybersex. Secondly, an Internet Usability Assessment serves as a prospective guide for future activities. That is, you can use a blank form to schedule alternative activities that are less conducive to computer use, such as going out to ballgame, going shopping, or spending time with a family member. Finally and most important for this exercise, you can use the log to identify high-risk situations or events that occur just prior to logging online, and you can evaluate the extent of any rationalizations you make to justify cybersex use. The next step is to analyze the results to make measurable changes in your current Internet practices.

2. Make Measurable Changes in Your Internet Behavior

As food addicts measure part of their recovery success through objective indicators such as reduced caloric intake and weight loss, cybersex addicts can objectively measure part of their recovery success through reduced online hours and abstinence from any contact with sexual online content. Based upon the results of your Internet Usability Assessment Form, determine how many hours per week you spend on the Internet and at which times you are most likely to surf. Perhaps you count twenty hours per week, spent mainly in the evenings while you are home alone at night. Or perhaps you spend thirty hours a week in a haphazard manner during the day, with no specific routine. Once you have taken an exhaustive inventory of your current Internet usage, consider the following ways to make measurable changes in your Internet behavior, focusing on abstinence from cybersex while being at the computer. As you proceed, continue to maintain a log of hourly changes in Internet use on the Internet Usability Assessment Form to calculate your level of progress.

- Establish structured Internet sessions that are programmed into part of your daily routine. Set reasonable time limits and goals pertaining to your computer use. For example, instead of your current twenty hours per week, set a new time limit of only ten hours per week. Then, schedule those ten hours in specific time slots and write them onto a calendar or weekly planner. Try to keep your Internet usage on a routine, weekly schedule to help maintain discipline and avoid future relapse. As an example of a ten-hour schedule, you might plan to use the Internet from 8 to 9 a.m. every morning to check your email, and then again from 4 to 5 p.m., just before you leave for the day. Incorporating a tangible daily and weekly schedule of Internet usage will give you a sense of being in control, rather than allowing the Internet to take control.

- Unlike television, the Internet doesn't have its own commercial breaks, so it's easy to lose track of time once you are online. Utilize external aids such as an alarm clock or an egg timer to put a break into your pattern of Net use. Predetermine the amount of time you will allot for each Internet session and preset an alarm that you keep near the computer. When it sounds, it means it is time to log off.

- Use another's Internet account to increase accountability of online actions.

- Determine new places to use the Internet that are more public and visible.

- Delete bookmarks of porn sites and files containing adult pictures.

- Apply filtering software such as NetNanny, CyberPatrol, or SurfControl to block access to adult web sites. The software will automatically and immediately shut down your web browser if you attempt to access adult material online. Many addicts describe the experience as a "cold shower" that breaks the momentum and snaps them out of their cybersex trance. Unfortunately, some cybersex addicts attempt to circumvent the software or simply uninstall it from the computer, only to find themselves more determined to return to their addiction. As one man put it, "I tried everything, but my urge for cybersex was just too strong. I am very clever and figured out all kinds of ways to get around the blocking software. It's like another challenge and really doesn't stop me. If anything, I waste more time trying to break the software than I did surfing for cybersex."

- Instead of using software that is easily disabled, switch to a family-friendly Internet Service Provider (ISP), such as Family.net, Mayberry USA, and Integrity Online, that completely removes all access to sexually explicit material from their servers, removing all temptation. The biggest benefit is that when you enroll in a new ISP, you gain a new Internet account with a new handle, which gives you a clean slate to make a fresh start with a new cyber-identity. One that hopefully will keep you on the path of abstinence and recovery. Whether you are considering filtering software or a new ISP, you ultimately must select the solution that best fits your lifestyle and work needs. And keep in mind, that just stopping cybersex with these techno-fixes is only part of the recovery process. You still must find healthy ways of coping with the underlying issues that brought you to cybersex in the first place.

3. Address How You will Deal with Abstinence

Recovery isn't a simple process, nor does it happen overnight. There will certainly be roadblocks and missteps along the way, so be patient with yourself. Keep in mind that throughout the entire process, and particularly in the early days of recovery, you will most likely experience a loss and miss being online for frequent periods of time. This is normal and should be expected. After all, for most addicts who derive a great source of pleasure from cybersex, living without it being a central part of one's life can be a very difficult adjustment.

Cybersex provide some measure of relief from discomfort, whether this is relief from anxiety, depression, loneliness, self-consciousness, or just a compulsive urge. Addiction clouds judgment, impairs insight, and numbs feelings. Abstinence, at least initially, causes psychological and even physical distress because you haven't developed alternative ways of dealing with those feelings. As an addict, if you stop using cybersex, you are essentially risking great distress such as increased irritability, moodiness, depression, anxiety, or anger. In this instance, it's easy to feel as if recovery is impossible. To help you transition into abstinence and maintain cybersex sobriety, I have outlined a plan that shows you how to *accept* responsibility for the behavior, *create* positive lifestyle changes, and *tackle* underlying issues that contributed to the addiction, which I call The ACT Plan.

Accept Responsibility for the Behavior

Cybersex addicts often have difficulty with cybersex sobriety because they are ambivalent about treatment. Initially, addicts go into therapy with mixed feelings because they have not taken full responsibility for the behavior and aren't sure if they really want to give it up. Part of the addict feels that cybersex is a healthy sexual outlet and rationalizes, "This isn't hurting anyone else," "Its no big deal," and "It is not the Internet, it is the stress in my life." And they minimize the hurt their behavior causes to loved ones: "Hey, it's just a machine," or "It's not really extramarital sex, it's just words on a screen." In some instances, the addict feels dragged into therapy by a spouse and begrudgingly enters treatment.

In the early days of therapy, Craig contradicted himself during our sessions. At first, he readily admitted to having an addiction. Then in the next session, he would minimize his behavior saying that it didn't cause any real damage and justified that it was okay to look at porn at work, because his boss would never find out. At times, he even blamed his wife for the addiction: "If we had sex more, I wouldn't need the Internet."

Unless you take ownership for your own problem, you can't expect that you will stick to sobriety from cybersex. It takes a daily commitment, especially if you do need to be at the computer, and if you aren't ready to make this commitment for yourself, and not for anyone else, then abstinence will be difficult to maintain. Admitting the problem and taking responsibility means owning your own feelings, understanding that only you can fix this, and holding yourself accountable for recovery. This is not to say that support and guidance from others isn't necessary. On the contrary, daily support from others is an instrumental part of the recovery process. But ultimately, recovery is about you taking charge of your own actions – and no one else can do that for you.

Create Positive Lifestyle Changes

Cybersex is a time-consuming activity, and to create more time for the computer, addicts neglect sleep, diet, exercise, hobbies, and socializing.

The initial loss of the cybersex activity means an increase in idle time or boredom, which only increases your temptation to surf, making it vital for you to find positive ways to fill the void created with the time now not spent at the computer. Here are some suggestions to create positive lifestyle changes that take you away from the computer and increase emotional and physical wellness:

- The time you have spent having cybersex might have replaced a once cherished activity or hobby. Perhaps you spend less time hiking, golfing, fishing, camping, or dating because of your Net use. Maybe you have stopped going to ball games, visiting the zoo, or volunteering at church. It's time to take a personal inventory of every practice that you have neglected or curtailed since your online habit emerged and rekindle your interest in the lost activities you once enjoyed.

- Cultivate alternative offline activities that are fulfilling and personally productive to fill the void created when you refrain from the Internet. Perhaps you have put off joining a fitness center or calling an old friend to arrange to have lunch – now is the time to go do it.

- Obtain spiritual fellowship in the form of personal prayer or pastoral counseling as part of your spiritual wellness and daily recovery.

- Practice daily mediation to focus your energy during recovery and improve your inner strength to fight temptation and relapse.

- Get proper rest.

- Improve your diet and overall physical fitness.

Tackle Underlying Issues

Addicts falsely assume that just stopping the behavior is enough to say, "I am recovered." But there is much more to full recovery than simply refraining from cybersex. Complete recovery means investigating the underlying issues that led up to the behavior and resolving them in a healthy manner; otherwise, relapse is likely to occur. As I have indicated, Cybersexual Addiction most likely stems from other emotional or situational problems such as depression, anxiety, stress, relationship troubles, career difficulties, impulse control problems, and/or childhood sexual abuse. While cybersex is a convenient distraction from these problems, it does very little to actually help you cope with the underlying issues that lead you to where you are today.

As I worked with Craig, we uncovered that he viewed himself as obsolete at his job and turned to cybersex to cope with his feelings: "I think a strong trigger has been reaching fifty. There is an underlying feeling that I have not accomplished as much as I would have liked with my life, and I have a younger work colleague who are very accomplished, so I kind of feel overwhelmed about competing in this environment. Of course, spending time in the Internet just makes things much, much worse. I used to be the top guy here, but now, it seems that these young hotshots are making more money and moving up faster. The more stressed and overwhelmed I become, the more I retreat to the cyber-porn, which only makes me more behind in my work. I come in on weekends to catch up or even stay late, only to be tempted again by the computer, and I hate myself for all the wasted time when I should be working."

As we can see with Craig, cybersex becomes a way for the addict to self-medicate in order to temporarily run away from life's problems. Over time, however, this coping mechanism proves to be unproductive and potentially harmful, as the issues hidden by the addictive behavior culminate into larger and larger problems. Addicts are most likely to use cybersex to cope with problems in the following ways:

1. Cybersex addicts feel tense, lonely, restless, depressed, withdrawn, angry, or worthless and use cybersex to wash away these feelings and temporarily feel confident, well liked, proud, or in love.

2. Cybersex addicts perceive themselves as undesirable and use cybersex to boost their self-esteem.

3. Cybersex addicts perceive their own sexual needs as immoral or deviant and use cybersex to validate their sexual urges.

4. Cybersex addicts have difficulty forming intimate relationships with others and hide behind the anonymity of cyberspace to connect with others in a non-threatening way.

5. Cybersex addicts often suffer from multiple addictions such as overeating, smoking, alcoholism, drug use, and compulsive gambling, and their addiction is an extension of underlying compulsive tendencies.

6. Cybersex addicts use the activity to escape turbulence in their careers or relationships.

Confronting the problem head on is the best way to approach it. If you are dealing with low self-esteem or depression, find healthier ways of dealing with your feelings. If you are having relationship troubles, enter couples counseling instead of turning to cybersex to address those intimacy issues. If you view porn at work to handle job stress, learn more effective stress management techniques to help you relax instead of relying on the Internet. If you suffer from multiple addictions, seek out professional guidance, where appropriate, to recognize the decision chain that leads to a lapse before it actually occurs. If you are having career troubles, investigate new job options or career paths. Of course, corrective behavior is easier said then done.

However, unresolved feelings or situations will only resurface over time and erode the success you have made as part of your abstinence program. For example, Craig repeatedly relapsed because he still didn't deal with his feelings about his career. Each time the company hired another young recruit, his underlying feelings of resentment surfaced and he relapsed into cybersex. Each time a same-aged friend announced his early retirement, his feelings of failure emerged and he relapsed again.

When he was young, Craig wanted to pursue acting, but his parents discouraged him because they felt that wasn't a legitimate career. As a result, he always regretted not pursuing his dream. As part of his recovery, Craig joined a community theater group that produced local plays. Initially, he took small acting roles that led to bigger and bigger roles, and as time allowed he helped with the set design and stage lighting. Craig's interest in cybersex diminished as he spent much of his free time at the theater – not to mention that he was finally doing something he loved.

Whatever the situation, confronting the issues that drove you towards addiction will not be easy, but it is the only way to achieve the personal growth necessary to maintain long-term recovery.

4. Understand the Sexual Needs that Drive the Addiction

As I described in Chapter 3, what drives a large part of the addiction is the ability for cybersex to fulfill unmet sexual needs or desires missing in the user's current sexual practices. In order to avoid relapse, you must identify the underlying sexual needs being met through cybersex and investigate ways to transfer meeting those needs into offline sexual behavior.

For example, Craig is normally shy, and has trouble initiating sex with his wife, but online, his entire sexual persona changed during cybersex: "I am into kinky sex with younger women, older women, black women - you name it. I just want the next sexual conquest," he explains. "I get really excited if she tells me about a new position that I haven't thought of before, if she likes being tied up, or if she is a virgin that I can deflower. I just love when I discover it is some horny teen that has never had real-life sex. Even if they lie, it's the fantasy of it. I want to be the first in my mind. Or tie up the older ones who need a real man. Most women know me as a kind-hearted chap, but I really want to dominate women, to take control, to use them. And this is my way of doing it."

Identify Underlying Sexual Needs

Ask yourself: What sexual needs does cybersex fulfill? Does cybersex give you sexual power, but offline, do you still fear sexual intimacy with your mate? Does cybersex make you feel better about your body, but offline do you still need to turn the lights off during sex? Does cybersex turn you into a cybervixen, but offline do you still have trouble initiating sex with your partner? Can you say things to online lovers that you can't say to your husband or wife?

Instead of using cybersex to avoid difficult feelings, it's time to figure out why sex isn't working in your life. The walls have already been somewhat broken down because you partly dealt with these feelings when online. For instance, Craig explored the impact of being raised in an Irish Catholic family, where he learned that sex was a duty to procreate and that masturbation is a sin. He realized that these negative messages still played in his mind today, making him feel guilty and ashamed of his sexuality. Online, he was able to absorb himself so fully in the online experience and how cyber-women made him feel sexually powerful that he forgot about his sexual inhibitions allowing him to control them. Craig's family dynamics also contributed to his sexual inadequacies. His mother was overly domineering with the family, and he perceived his father to be weak. In one of our sessions, Craig admitted that he resented his father for not being stronger and hated his mother for her dominance. In a flash of insight, Craig realized that cybersex helped him rebel against those religious messages of his youth, and his powerful online persona helped him to feel superior to his father. Also, his sexual control of cyber-women helped him to unleash his underlying anger towards women. With greater insight, Craig understood how his religion and family upbringing impacted his sexual development, and he was able to process and confront these issues using healthier sexual outlets.

As you work towards recovery, keep in mind that this level of self-analysis is long-term and intensive, and you must be prepared for the changes that occur as you explore these highly personal sexual feelings.

Transfer Positive Qualities

Once you have identified the unmet sexual needs that cybersex fills, the next step is to discover ways to generalize that behavior into real-life sexual situations. The more you can integrate cybersex behavior into your current sexual practices, the less likely you will rely upon cybersex as a substitute for what is missing. For instance, Craig was able to easily and aggressively initiate sex with women online, but at home, he still had difficulty initiating sex with his wife. Online, he was confident in his lovemaking skills, but in bed with his wife, he was terrified to touch her. In therapy, we developed specific goals to help Craig connect his online world with his marital relationship. Craig was more honest in therapy about his sexual fears and in the process of telling his wife his true feelings, the couple grew closer and more intimate, which helped Craig feel safer initiating sex with his wife. Her continued receptivity to his sexual advances helped him to overcome his inhibitions and build new confidence. Mental imagery also helped Craig to feel more comfortable during sex. As he approached his wife for sex, he imagined how domineering and aggressive he felt when online. Picturing these feelings, he was able to further transfer his sexual prowess online into a sexual relationship with his wife.

5. Develop a Proactive Plan to Deal with High-Risk Situations

Learn to avoid high-risk situations and plan in advance how these might be avoided or successfully coped with. High-risk situations vary among addicts. Some find that movies with erotic scenes, stress in a marriage, arguments with children, or job pressures trigger cravings for cybersex, while others find any moments of idle time is enough to trigger cravings. Minimizing exposure to the Internet as much as possible is a proactive way to prevent you from returning to old cybersex habits during these vulnerable moments. For most addicts, this translates into limiting all extracurricular use of the Internet and eliminating tasks that can just as easily be performed offline. Instead of buying a book on Amazon.com, go to your local bookseller. Instead of reading *The New York Times* online, read the actual newspaper. Instead of playing computer solitaire, buy a pack of cards and play offline.

When you must go online for legitimate purposes, prioritize the online tasks that need to be performed during each Internet session in order to focus your activities and reduce the temptation to randomly surf, which only increases the risk of relapse. Before logging onto the Internet, prepare a list of specific tasks that need to be accomplished online and stick to that list as you use the Internet. A sample task list might look like the following:

1. *Check email using MS Outlook Express*
2. *Send file attachment to a co-worker using MS Outlook Express.*

3. *Process vendor orders on PurchasePro.com for new project at work.*

4. *Look up real time stock quotes on E-trade.com*

Notice that the list outlines both the nature of the task to be performed, such as "check email" or "look up stock quotes," and it specifies the exact web location to complete the event, such as "MS Outlook Express" or "E-Trade.com." In the same way bringing a grocery list with you to do the food shopping helps eliminate extraneous purchases, prioritizing online tasks helps eliminate extraneous web surfing that might lead to a relapse. Without a grocery list, there is a greater temptation to buy items on impulse that you really don't need. Without an online list, there is a greater temptation to click onto sexually explicit online material.

6. Correct the Rationalizations that Leads to Relapse

Most cybersex addicts engage in a self-destructive internal dialogue of rationalizations that serve to onset relapse. The pattern begins with rationalizing the behavior followed by regret and temporary abstinence, until the negative thinking that justifies cybersex use creeps back into the addict's mind, triggering relapse. I refer to this process as the **Stop-Start Relapse Cycle** and it falls into four main stages:

1. *Rationalization* – The addict rationalizes that cybersex serves as a "treat" from a long, hard day of work, often making self-statements such as, "I work hard, I deserve it," "Just a few minutes won't hurt," "I can control my Net use," or "Cybersex relaxes me," or "My sex drive is stronger than my partner's, so its okay." The addict justifies the need to look at a few pictures or chat for a few minutes, but soon discovers that time slips by and the behavior is not so easily contained.

2. *Regret* – After the cybersexual experience, the addict experiences a period of deep regret. After the climax, the addict realizes that work is piling up and feels guilty for the behavior making

statements such as, "I know this is hurting my job," "I can't believe I wasted all this time," or "I am a horrible person for what I just did."

3. *Abstinence* – The addict views the behavior as a personal failure of willpower and promises never to do it again, so a short period of abstinence follows. During this time, he temporarily engages in healthy patterns of behavior, works diligently, resumes interests in old hobbies, spends more time with his family, exercises, and gets enough rest.

4. *Relapse* – The addict begins to crave and miss cybersex, as temptations to return to cybersex emerge during stressful or emotionally charged moments. The addict recalls the self-medicating effects of cybersex and its associated relaxation and excitement. The addict remembers how good cybersex felt and forgets how bad it feels afterwards. Soon, the rationalization period starts again, and the availability of the computer easily starts the cycle anew.

For example, Craig explains how the Start-Stop Relapse Cycle led to his frequent struggle with relapse. "I always think about cybersex when I feel stressed from work and overwhelmed on the job," he says. "I always promise to only do it for a half an hour or an hour, but time just slips by. Each time I log off after cybersex, I promise myself that I will never do it again. I hate myself for all the wasted time I spent online and quickly try to catch up on the lost work. I go a few weeks, then the pressure seems to build up inside. I play mind games with myself, telling myself just a little won't hurt. No one will know what I am doing. Sometimes I actually believe that I am in control, but then I wear myself down and the whole process starts all over again, and I feel defeated that I will never get rid of these feelings."

To break this pattern, you need to attack the initial rationalizations that launch the entire Stop-Start Relapse Cycle, using distraction techniques, reminder cards, and steps to exaggerate the addiction.

Distraction – Rationalizations may be triggered by a cybersex addict's response to stress, tension, boredom, loneliness, sexual arousal, or working in a cue-laden environment (such as using the same computer for work that you use for cybersex). To combat rationalizations, distraction helps you to refocus your attention away from these thoughts and feelings to prevent relapse. Recite a poem or a prayer. Concentrate on your surroundings, such as your office setting or the views outside your window, and describe what you see. The more you can focus and give details of these external events, the less likely you will focus on your internal urges. Or ask yourself, "What advice would I give my best friend if he or she were in this situation right now?" Sometimes, the opportunity to give yourself advice as if it were another person redirects your attention and helps you to stop the maladaptive thoughts that lead to relapse. Finally, physically remove yourself from the computer - take a break, perform household chores, visit a friend, call your spouse, or go for a drive.

Reminder Cards – This next exercise is designed to help increase your motivation to avoid relapse by emphasizing the adverse consequences of using and recognizing the benefits of not using. Make a list of the five major problems caused by cybersex in your life. Then, generate a parallel list of the five major benefits for cutting down on your overall Internet use or abstaining from cybersex. It is well worth it to make your lists as broad and all encompassing as possible. For example, Craig's list looked like this:

Benefits:

    1. More quality time and intimacy with spouse.

    2. Greater attention towards my children.

    3. More time for enhanced family relations.

    4. Better job performance.

    5. Raise or promotion at work.

67

Problems:

1. *Divorce from my spouse.*

2. *Conflicts with extended family.*

3. *Loss of my children.*

4. *Problems at work and distance from coworkers.*

5. *Potential job termination if I am caught.*

Next, transfer the two lists onto a 3x5 index card and post the card at your computer. If you utilize more than one computer workstation, or if posting the card would draw unwarranted attention (e.g., at work among co-workers), then simply keep the card in a pants or coat pocket, purse, or wallet. Take out the index card as a reminder of what you need to avoid and what you need to do when the rationalizations begin. As a means to increase motivation and commitment, review the index card several times a week to reflect on the problems created by cybersex in your life and the benefits of controlling your use.

Exaggerate the Behavior - If you are having problems generating your list of consequences, try to exaggerate the addiction. When smokers frequently relapse, smoking cessation groups often recommend they exaggerate their smoking habit. For instance, if they normally smoke a pack a day, they are told to smoke three packs a day. The theory is "Smoke until you are sick of smoking" so that cigarettes become associated with a sore throat, weak lungs, shallow breath, and an ugly taste in the smoker's mouth.

This same technique is an effective tool for reflection and relapse prevention of Cybersexual Addiction. Instead of spending your typical few hours a day for cybersex, take a whole day and do it to excess. Even if you want to stop, keep going. If you have something else you should be doing, make yourself stay on the computer. In other words, make yourself "Have cybersex until you are sick of cybersex." After one of these deliberate binges, when you start to get bored or frustrated with the online activity, write down the experience. Try to capture the full impact of how boring it became, how worried you were about being caught, how drained you felt, how your muscles ached at being stationary at the computer, how your eyes got blurry, or how much time you wasted. This exercise not only makes you sick of cybersex, but it helps you generate a consequence list so that when the rationalizations begin, such as, "Just one more time won't hurt" you are armed and ready to combat those thoughts. And remember, if you do slip along the way, encourage yourself to look at these incidents as opportunities for learning.

7. Find Sponsorship and Continued Support

Like many cybersex addicts, when Craig realized that he had a problem, he was afraid to seek out help for fear that his wife would discover his secret online life. He initially tried to deal with the problem on his own by restricting his Internet use and canceling his subscriptions to several of the pornography sites. However, each time he tried to refrain from the activity, he was back to his old habits within weeks.

Cybersex addicts believe that everyone will abandon them if they knew the truth and instinctively fear that their sexual behavior is so bad, it would disgust others. In reality, I find that loved ones already suspect that something is wrong, and continued secrecy over the long run damages trust in your relationships more than telling the truth. Honesty stops the addict from hiding the behavior and breaks the power of the secret life.

Explore ways that family and friends can play a sponsorship role

Involving loved ones in the recovery process can be a rich source of nurturing and sponsorship to help you maintain abstinence. Once Craig finally mustered the courage and strength to admit his addiction to cybersex to his wife, much to his surprise, she was relieved to finally learn the truth and offered comfort, support, and encouragement to help him overcome his addiction. They are both devote Christians and when Craig felt the urge to go back to cybersex, he and his wife prayed together to fight the temptation. Through the process, they were able to build a stronger and more spiritual relationship. Learning that loved ones can accept mistakes and human infallibility takes a tremendous pressure off the addict and allows him to gain the support necessary for continued cybersex sobriety.

Amend Old Relationships

Due to their addiction, cybersex addicts often hurt or lose significant real-life relationships, such as a spouse, a parent, or a close friend. Often, these were individuals who provided the addict with support, love, and acceptance before the Internet came into his life, and their absence only makes the addict feel worthless and reinforces past notions that they are unlovable. Therefore, it is essential for the addict to amend and reestablish these broken relationships to achieve recovery and find the support necessary to fight the addiction. Clearly, making amends won't be easy because of the hurt and pain caused by the addictive behavior, and it takes great courage to admit wrongdoing and ask forgiveness. However, it is important for you to openly acknowledge personal failure and correct past mistakes in order for genuine forgiveness to be received. With this type of sincerity, it is possible to rebuild closeness and intimacy.

Foster New Relationships

This is also a time to foster new social outlets that provide opportunities to make contact with others in meaningful ways, such as getting involved with local church groups, service organizations, and community activities. Forming new relationships not only helps maintain abstinence as outside involvement takes you away from the computer, but this diminishes the social isolation created by the addiction.

RECOVERY CHECKLIST

To help in the recovery process, I have summarized the issues in this convenient checklist that you can use to maintain your motivation and reinforce healthy Internet behavior.

1. **Assess Your Current Internet Use Practices:**

   a. Carefully examine the extent of your current use cycle and its associated problems.

   b. Identify online applications that are the most problematic and trigger abuse.

   c. Look for specific situations in which you are most vulnerable.

2. **Make Measurable Changes in Your Internet Behavior:**

   a. Maintain a log of hourly changes in Internet use.

   b. Determine new places to use the Internet that are more public and visible.

   c. Utilize technology-based solutions to maintain cybersex abstinence when cravings occur.

3. **Address How You Will Deal with Abstinence:**

   a. Identify your current struggles and how will you cope with the emotional and physical losses you may experience when restraining from cybersex.

   b. Be proactive in lifestyle modifications that take you away from the computer.

   c. Tackle the underlying issues that led you to the addiction in the first place.

4. **Understand the Sexual Needs that Drive the Addiction:**

   a. Understand the unmet needs that cybersex once filled in your life and find alternative ways of coping to prevent relapse.

   b. Transfer the positive qualities of cybersex into healthier sexual outlets.

   c. Explore and resolve underlying sexual feelings before they resurface into a relapse.

5. Develop a Proactive Plan to Deal with High-Risk Situations:

a. Learn to avoid high-risk situations.

b. Plan in advance how these might be avoided or successfully coped with.

c. Minimize deliberate exposure to cybersex-related triggers or situations. Be ready to identify unforeseeable "accidental exposure" to the Internet and be prepared for how to cope with the situation.

6. Correct the Rationalizations that Lead to Relapse:

a. Learn about your relapse interpretations: "I blew it this time, I guess I will never stop, so I will just keep using."

b. Watch out for internal "entitlement" themes, such as "I had a hard day, I deserve to cyber" or "Well, I was productive today, so cybersex will be my treat."

c. Encourage yourself to look at slips as isolated incidents that can be conceived of as opportunities for learning.

7. Find Sponsorship and Continued Support:

a. Discuss ways that friends and family can assist in your recovery

b. Amend old relationships and foster new relationships.

c. If you don't enlist help from others, then ask yourself how you will abstain from cybersex without accountability to someone.

SIGNS OF HEALTHY INTERNET USE

The final step is to give yourself credit for your efforts, even if you do relapse once in a while. Get back on the horse and just start again. Because using the computer for work is often part of your daily routine, it may not be easy to detect when you have you have made progress. To help you recognize achievement towards your recovery goals, I have listed the following ten signs of healthy cybersex use:

1. You stick to your schedule of Internet use and don't eclipse your targeted number of total hours online each week.

2. Your spouse, parent, or other loved one tells you they see the difference in your Internet habits and your behavior toward them.

3. You keep a strict accounting of the money you spend for online service fees, especially for adult web sites, and stay within your budget.

4. You perform work tasks in a timely fashion that closely resembles your pattern before turning to addictive cybersex use.

5. You rediscover those favorite hobbies and activities you used to enjoy.

6. You expend greater energy communicating with those directly in front of you than to strangers on the Net.

7. You see others obsessed with cybersex in a different light, with an understanding that they're creating problems for themselves and those closest to them.

8. When you do use the Internet for legitimate reasons, you feel less and less tempted to resume your old habits.

9. You feel a greater desire to go out with your spouse or family and socialize with friends, turning down fewer invitations and making more of your own.

10. You look back at your time of addiction to cybersex and see a different person from a different period of time.

CHAPTER 5

INFIDELITY ONLINE: HOPE AND HELP FOR COUPLES DEALING WITH CYBERAFFAIRS

"My partner and I responded to a domestic dispute. When we arrived, the husband was beating on the bedroom door with his fists, demanding that his wife let him inside. At first, I thought his wife was in bed with another man. I was shocked to discover that the wife was alone, chatting on the computer with her online boyfriend, and she had locked the husband out of the room because he threatened to take the computer away from her."

A Police Officer from Pennsylvania

What actually constitutes adultery over the Internet? Is flirting online cheating? Are online romances cheating? Is having cybersex and sharing your sexual fantasies with someone online cheating? To approach these questions, our moral views and opinions guide the answers, formed less by fact, and more based upon our social conventions, religious teachings, family upbringing, books, and life experiences. Not surprisingly, the Catholic Church views all cybersex as cheating, according to Famiglia Cristiana (Christian Family), a magazine close to the Vatican,[1] "Adultery is adultery, even if it's virtual, it is just as sinful as the real thing." On the other end of the spectrum, perhaps if we asked Bill Clinton these questions, we must first define what is meant by the word *is*.

To personalize the situation, I typically ask, "How would you feel if it were your significant other engaged in an online affair?" And most folks reply that they would not like it. Unlike affairs that occur in the physical world, online affairs are based upon the fantasy of what reality will look like. Ultimately, each person and each couple must decide where to draw the distinction between fantasy and cheating. However, as the following case shows, when it comes to online liaisons, virtual fantasies have the power to distort the reality of a happy marriage by magnifying weaknesses in the relationship and making the marriage seem troubled in comparison to the intensity and excitement of a new online lover.

DANGEROUS COMPARISONS

Mary and Bob lived in Maine, and had been married for almost twenty-eight-years before they decided to buy a home computer so that Bob could learn how to trade stocks online. Instead of Bob using the computer for investing, Mary started to take it over nightly to play in chat rooms. Within weeks, she became emotionally involved with several new cyber-friends and their needs often took place over her husband and her family. In her new virtual life, she met Hank, a divorced businessman from Texas, who immediately became her closest online friend. She opened up to Hank about her hopes and dreams for the future more than she was able to do with her husband.

She loved chatting with Hank and hated to be away from the computer. She woke up early just to see if Hank was online. She stayed up late at the computer, just to chat with him for hours upon hours. She felt as if Hank completely understood her every mood and desire. Mary pictured Hank as the perfect man. He was loving, caring, and romantic.

The more her relationship with Hank grew, the more she started to compare him to Bob. Hank seemed to be a dream man, who cared only about her, while Bob seemed to be a workaholic more centered on his career. Hank always seemed to say the right thing, while Bob seemed inattentive to her needs.

As she became more consumed with imagining a new life with Hank, all the little things that she used to ignore about Bob, like his dirty socks on the floor and his snoring, started to bother her. In her mind, she suddenly wondered if she was married to the right person. Mary started to feel as if the passion in her marriage had died a long time ago and questioned if starting a new life with Hank wouldn't make her happier. At the same time Mary was questioning her marriage, Bob became increasingly angry and argumentative about how much time she spent at the computer, and even threatened to cancel the Internet service, causing more distance in their marriage.

Meanwhile, online, Hank expressed how much he loved her and wanted her to move to Texas to be with him. Even though Mary had only known Hank for five months and mainly spoke to him through typed online conversations, and a few long distance telephone calls, she fell deeply in love with him and decided to leave her husband. Hank arranged to pay for a plane ticket so that Mary could fly down to Texas from Maine, and while Bob was at work, Mary packed her bags and left her husband a goodbye note on the kitchen table.

Unfortunately, scenarios like this are suddenly plaguing more and more couples today and neither they nor their counselors are adequately prepared to deal with this new digital temptation. Consider a husband living in New York who believes it is harmless to flirt with a woman in a chat room who lives in another part of the world because, prior to surfing cyberspace, physical distance meant that nothing would actually happen between the people involved. Picture a wife who rationalizes that having cybersex isn't really infidelity because, in the past, the lack of physical contact meant that such fantasies, like her fantasies about movie stars, would never be realized.

But as Mary's case illustrates, even if an online affair is never consummated in the physical world, "words on a screen" create havoc on a couple's stability and trust that can ultimately lead to separation and divorce. Each week, I receive phone calls, emails, and letters from men and women whose relationships ended because of online sexual liaisons. At social gatherings, I often hear about a husband or wife running off with someone they met on the computer. I am constantly talking with therapists who are treating more and more couples wounded by virtual infidelity. The problem has grown so much over the years, that online and offline support groups for "Cyberwidows" have been established to help betrayed partners victimized by online infidelity cope with their feelings of frustration, anger, abandonment, and confusion over the sudden end to what was perceived, as a once happy relationship.

If your relationship has just ended because of a cyberaffair, then the information in this chapter will show you that you are not alone and help you cope in the wake of starting a new life. If you are a couple who is trying to salvage your relationship despite the hurt caused by virtual adultery, the information in this chapter gives you specific communication tools to form a more loving and trusting relationship for the future. If you suspect that your partner is cheating online, the information in this chapter will help you identify the warning signs and point you in the right direction for help. Perhaps you are a couple that recently bought a new computer, or are contemplating buying one, then the information in this chapter will be especially important to prevent an online affair from brewing in the future.

First, I'll share a few of those messages I have received from cyberwidows. Here is a sampling of real e-mails, only the names are changed.

Dr. Dr. Young,

Please help me. I don't know where else to turn to cope with my husband's addiction to online sex chat rooms. I am pregnant with our second daughter and it is hard to keep up the good fight under these conditions. I love my husband. He is a good man with a bad disease. We are working on things together slowly but surely. If we didn't have kids I think I might have left him by now but they help to keep us together. We mutually love our kids enough to try and deal with this problem together instead of getting divorced and going that route. I still have enough in me to keep on trying but some days I feel like I just want to go somewhere alone and break down. I hate to see the suffering his disease causes him, me, and ultimately our family. I am determined not to let the illness win. A little advice or just a little strength would be greatly appreciated. Tonight I am sad because I am in one of my "I just want everything to be normal" moods.

Thank you for listening.

Karen

Dear Dr. Young,

I am currently going through a divorce and custody dispute in a case that is centered around my complaint that my wife had been addicted to computer sex. She engaged in assorted acts of sexual misconduct including cybersex, phone sex, and a series of sexual affairs (primarily one-night stands) with several different men met through the Internet during a six-month period. My primary concern is the mental well being of my 14-year-old son, who is now living with my wife. Although my wife is taking care of his physical needs, I feel her emotional and mental state will create long-term emotional problems for my son. Please help me to sort through these tough issues.

Ken

Dear Dr. Young,

I am at my wit's end. I discovered tons of email from a woman my husband met online. I just cried when I found it. Then I got mad, very mad. I wanted to smash the computer into pieces. I gave him an ultimatum, and told him that it was either me or her. And I stuck to my guns and was well prepared to leave. He promised to stop the relationship. It's been 6 weeks and he is showing signs of withdrawal: oversleeping, insomnia, crankiness, forgetfulness, forgets words while talking, strange eating patterns, and slight depression. As for me each time he goes to work, I wonder if he is really working as a systems administrator or chatting with her at work. All our trust is gone. I worry if he tries to chat with her when he is home alone. I won't let it go and constantly need to talk to him about it, which I realize isn't great for our relationship but I just don't know how else to cope with his behavior. We have been married for 17 years and raised one adopted child. I always thought we had a good marriage and a great sex life but now I feel like there are parts of him I don't know. Now I don't know if I can look at him the same way again.

Cindy

Dear Dr. Young,

My name is Mike and I am having a great deal of difficulty due to my wife's infatuation with AOL sex chat rooms. I am having trouble because she spends two or three hours every day having cybersex and neither of us have that much free time. I end up staying home with our 17 month old child until she can drag herself out of bed when I'm supposed to be at work, or most of the time I just "exist" in our house when the boy is asleep while she pounds away, unreachable, on the keyboard. I think this is cheating, and she says its just fantasy and not to worry, but it is driving me insane. I love my wife but can't tolerate her behavior nor treat our family like I am a single parent. I was wondering if you could e-mail me any information you have to help.

Mike

Dear Dr. Young,

I had to cancel our credit cards because I am afraid my wife will take all our money and run off with someone she met on the Net. We have four children and I can't believe how much her personality changed since she discovered cybersex with men. It is killing me. I am sick all the time, I find myself doing all the chores around the house, our children are neglected and no matter what I say, she ignores my requests to stop it. Before the Internet, we were good Christians, went to church, and did a great deal with our family. She was a wonderful wife and mother, but now I feel like I am living with a stranger. I never thought something like this could happen to us. I mean she will be online until 3 a.m., and sometimes spends up to 16 hours a day chatting with this man. I know they had phone sex because I discovered the phone bills and I think she is even arranging to meet him. I don't believe it is love, but it is sex. The cybersex chat logs I found between them are disgusting. I don't even know this woman anymore.

Bill

THE DAMAGE DONE BY ONLINE INFIDELITY

Cyberaffairs are complex and not always about romance. Online infidelity can take on several forms ranging from romantic online liaisons to random hot sex chat encounters to interactive web cam sex. Whether these virtual infidelities are realized in the physical world or not, the emotional after affects can lead to several significant problems among committed couples.

Betrayal and Broken Trust

The jealousy, hurt, and betrayal caused by an online affair are just as real as if the affair had occurred in the physical world. For example, Shelia is a sixty-eight-year-old woman who recently became widowed when her husband of forty-three-years died suddenly from a heart attack. After his death, she was cleaning out his computer to give it to her granddaughter, when she discovered reams of emails from a woman he met online. Her emails described in graphic detail how she wanted to make love with him and his email replies to her were just as erotic and steamy. Shelia cried as she read through each email and wondered how the man she thought of as her best friend for all of these years could have done this to her. She felt angry, confused, and questioned if she ever knew him at all. As Shelia grieved his death, all she could do cope with the betrayal alone.

Secrecy and lies are necessary to maintain an online affair that over time erode and eventually destroy a couple's trust.[2] A wife starts to make excuses for why she needs to be online all night long. A husband lies about what he does on the computer saying it is "for work," when he is really chatting with women online. Soon, small white lies add up to bigger and bolder lies to conceal a secret online life.

In this situation, a partner starts to wonder what he does on the computer all night. A suspicious partner may try to discuss feelings of uncertainty and confusion, only to be met with anger, verbal attacks, or defensiveness by a loved one denying the affair. This may force suspicious partners to play "detective" in order to discover the truth, often confirming their worst fears. A husband tries to break the password on the computer, only to read erotic email sent by his wife to strange online men. A wife may rifle through her husband's wallet looking for clues, only to discover strange women's phone numbers accompanied by several calling cards. In fact, Elizabeth Field, a finance manager at a Chicago car dealership, launched Infidelitybusters.com because she knew of increasing numbers of people who have been burned by virtual cheating. The site's premise is simple – as long as the suspected cheater uses AOL, all that's needed is a screen name and a simple profile, including hobbies, race, and age. "It's just little things, so I can create my profile to match theirs," explains Field.

Once she has received the information, Field goes online and attempts to lure the suspected cheater into a compromising position. "I'll Instant Message the person with a pick-up line like, 'Hey, nice profile'" Field said. If the suspect bites, Field will push further and further until she gets her target to agree to a meeting. That's when she presents her client with the evidence she's amassed. Oftentimes, the client isn't really surprised when he or she gets the bad news, but the actual proof provides a sense of closure.

In other cases, discovering the true nature of a partner's virtual affairs can come as a great shock, as one wife explains, "I was unprepared to learn the truth, especially after twenty-two years of marriage. My husband has been meeting men in chat rooms and they phone each other and mutually masturbate. He says he's not bisexual or gay - he says he only does it out of curiosity and boredom. How can I ever believe him? Has anyone else suffered this kind of shock? I am going crazy and I have no one to talk to. For the sake of my children, my life is running on auto-pilot at the moment. I am so confused and hurt. He even placed an online ad of his own, but when I found out about it he deleted it. I fear this is more than just a fantasy, and he wants to have a real live affair with a man in our area."

Changes in the Couple's Sex Life

Spouses often rationalize that their online sexual flirtations are harmless fun and may even believe that their online infidelities actually help their marriage by preventing them from running out to have an affair in the physical world. As one husband explains, "My wife feels like sex

81

twice a week is enough for her, but I need it more often than that. When I discovered cybersex, it was a way to get my needs met without hurting my wife." However, in reality, virtual sex does harm and interfere with a couple's sex life, possibly to the point that computer-based fantasies replace the desire to be with a spouse or partner.[3, 4] As a partner becomes increasingly interested in the virtual world, noticeable changes in his lovemaking frequency and/or quality become evident in the relationship and he may begin to:

- Make excuses to avoid sex (e.g., I am not in the mood, too tired, working too hard, the children might hear, my back hurts too much).
- Feel distant and emotionally detached when making love.
- Appear self-focused and only interested only in his pleasure.
- Blame a partner for not being good in bed.
- Ask his partner to participate in sexual activities that the other person finds repulsive or objectionable.
- Lose all interest in sex and stop initiating sex.

For example, one wife describes how her husband's online affairs impacted their sexual relationship. "My husband was online having sex with multiple and meaningless people, yet he was destroying our marriage over this virtual fantasy life," she explains. "He believes that it isn't cheating because he doesn't get involved in a "relationship" with any of these online women. He rationalizes that this is just fantasy, like watching a movie. But our sex life has become intolerable. At night, he wakes me up at two or three in the morning for sex after having hot sex chat with these women. If that isn't bad enough, he then returns to the computer for more cybersex when we are done. I resent the computer and hate having sex with him now. My husband used to be a tender lover and liked sensual foreplay, now he is mechanical and distant. I feel repelled and disgusted by his actions, and I just wish I could have my loving husband back in my arms."

Physical Adultery

Virtual adultery is a doorway that can lead to physical adultery. Unlike looking at an adult magazine or watching an X-rated movie, fantasizing with an online lover involves a real person on the other end of a computer screen, creating an opportunity for an offline relationship to develop. Cyberspace abounds with chat rooms, such as "Married and Cheating," "Horny Wife for Affair," or "Hubby Needs Mistress," that facilitate meeting a potential people for an online or offline affair. Inside these chat rooms, online lovers are often also married, which serves to normalize the adulterous behavior. Cyber-lovers fantasize about real-life meetings for sexual pleasure and describe what they would do if they met in person. The fantasy becomes more ingrained and the idea of actually meeting becomes reinforced with repeated chats and/or telephone conversations. A husband may rationalize, "My wife won't find out" or a wife justifies meeting her cyberlover, "I am not satisfied with our sex life anyway." Soon their urges circumvent good judgment, and they plan to meet for an offline rendezvous to carry out what they can only imagine online.

Separation and Divorce

Over time, online affairs become more time-consuming and costly. Eventually, the secret life of the user is discovered or uncovered and the couple experiences a tremendous crisis. Often, the husband or wife engaged in the online affair will then enter a period of extreme remorse, beg for forgiveness, and promise never to act out again. His promises at the time are probably sincere, and most loved ones want to believe the words. A honeymoon period may follow, including intense sexual activity between the couple. Since sex is often regarded as a sign of love, a spouse may be lulled into believing everything is really all right, offer forgiveness, and bind up her wounded spirit and go on. She is later shattered to discover that the unaccounted time and secrecy has returned. If the core issues aren't addressed, relapse is bound to happen. And if acting out sexually online continues, then the whole process can lead to separation and even divorce.

In the past decade, the court system has seen an increase in the number of divorce cases prompted by virtual adultery. My initial survey on Internet addiction in 1996 revealed that 53% of the 596 people I surveyed indicated that online infidelities lead to marital separation and divorce.[5] In my clinical practice, I have personally witnessed marriages of fifteen, twenty, or twenty-five years end because of brief cyber-fling. Even the American Academy of Matrimonial Lawyers has reportedly seen an increase in the number of new divorce cases prompted by cyberaffairs.[6]

Domestic Violence

The jealousy a spouse feels about the affair can turn into anger, rage, and even violence. In a recent headline-making story, a wife took a machete to her husband's computer after she discovered that he was having cybersex with online women. Instead of attacking the computer, an angry spouse can attack the person having the online affair. For example, I recently received a call from an Emergency Room physician who wanted a consult on a domestic violence case. Initially, I wasn't sure why he had contacted me, until he explained the husband had beaten the wife when he discovered reams of erotic email, naked pictures of men, and strange men's phone numbers on the family computer.

Across the country, domestic violence counselors and law enforcement agents are seeing a rise in the number of assault and battery cases prompted by online infidelities. Recently, a police officer friend confided in me, "My partner and I responded to a domestic dispute. When we arrived, the husband was beating on the bedroom door with his fists, demanding that his wife let him inside. At first, I thought his wife was in bed with another man. I was shocked to discover that the wife was alone, chatting on the computer with her online boyfriend, and she had locked the husband out of the room because he threatened to take the computer away from her."

THE IMPACT OF VIRTUAL INFIDELITY ON CHILDREN

At an alarming rate, I receive a growing number of cries for help from children whose parents are engaged in an online affair. Here is part of one

84

such letter I received from a son about his mother: "I need your help. I am sixteen and discovered that my mom is cheating on my father online. She's in her late 40s and pretends to be in her early 20s when she has cybersex with online guys. This issue has finally come to a climax with me because I want it to stop, yet I don't know how. It is ruining our relationship and things have currently become extremely ugly. My mother isn't a bad person, to say the least, but she is just doing something wrong. I have no idea if I should tell my dad or confront her or what. I don't have any money, though I wish I did because she and the rest of us need help abolishing this addiction that is taking her away from us."

Because children are often more computer-savvy than their parents, they are more likely to be the first one in the family to discover mom's online affair or dad's secret online pornography collection. Children who use a parent's computer can accidentally find undeleted emails, locked files, old chat logs, or history folders that reveal the true nature about what a parent does online. And when that child makes this discovery, he or she is deeply wounded and thinks, "How can my mom or dad do this?"

Children are sensitive, especially over matters that concern their parents. In many respects, children grow up with this belief that mommy and daddy will stay together forever, and it is often very traumatic for a son or daughter to learn that a parent has had an affair, even if it is virtual. The discovery of a parent's erotic online escapades can shock and devastate a child, and a child may develop feelings of deep anger at the adulterous parent for having the affair and for breaking the family apart.

Not only does this discovery cause emotional pain, but that child may develop sleep and eating problems and become increasing depressed as she or he internally agonizes about what to do: "Should I tell my father my mom is having cybersex?" "Should I confront my mom directly?" "How should I tell I found out without her hating me?" "How can I keep my parent's marriage from falling apart?" "My mom wants to run away with her cyberboyfriend, how can I stop her?" A son or daughter also feels too embarrassed to talk with friends about it, so he or she ends up feeling alone in his or her pain and confusion. If you happen to be a son or daughter reading this book now, here are three important steps to consider:

(1)　Do not attempt to handle this all by yourself.

(2)   Avoid taking sides with either parent until you learn all the facts.

(3)   Talk with a relative, trusted family friend, school counselor, or teacher about the situation for their guidance.

BECOMING AN ENABLER

Many spouses don't know how to react to something that seems to be a fantasy. Unlike having an affair at the office or picking someone up at a singles bar, cyberaffairs *start* in the couple's home, typically through the family computer. And unlike like offline adultery, that might take months or years to develop, a cyberaffair happens suddenly, sometimes within days or weeks of getting online, creating immediate changes in a partner's behavior. The partner engaged in the online affair suddenly is preoccupied with the Internet, demands privacy at the computer, ignores routine chores, and is emotionally distant from family members. Within months, a spouse asks for a divorce to run away with a new friend cyber-lover.

The abandoned spouse is left dazed and confused. How can he be in love after just a few months of chatting? How can he destroy our family for someone he's never met? The abandoned spouse feels as if it is a phase and believes the person will eventually snap out of it. So she waits, in hopes that he will come to his senses and their lives will return to normal, however, that rarely happens. Online affairs, even if never consummated in the physical world, change a couple's life forever. In their attempt to save the relationship, partners panic, and will do almost anything to save the relationship, even to the extreme of enabling the online affair.

Enabling behavior is passive behavior that supports the online affair. Enablers tend to be those who's self-esteem comes from their success as people-pleasers. Their main goal in life is to give their partners what they want at the expense of their own needs. To assure success at pleasing, the enabler may become extremely sensitive to the momentary mood of his or her partner, constantly worrying about what the partner thinks and trying extremely hard not to make a mistake. Because of these self-defeating characteristics, the enabler usually is much more in tune with what someone else wants than with his or her own wants and needs, and the person's core belief is that "I am unlovable."

An enabling wife may engage in a variety of behaviors that range from the smallest violation of her value system to the truly dangerous and destructive. The energy expended on such an endeavor can take a heavy emotional toll, as she tries repeatedly and unsuccessfully to "keep her man happy." She may change her hair color, lose or gain weight, quit her job or go to work, or wear sexy underwear. Or she may perform sex acts that are unpleasant or repulsive to her, or attend events that shock and confuse her, swing with others, or expose herself to sexually transmitted diseases. Or, if children are involved, she may use them and/or ignore them in her efforts to focus on her self-absorbed husband. She may even rationalize his behavior and put undo pressure on herself for not trying hard enough, with self-statements, such as:

- I am not woman enough for him.

- At least he isn't out drinking.

- At least he isn't beating me.

- Virtual sex is better than having an actual affair.

- I could never please him sexually.

- Maybe there is something wrong with me.

- Maybe I am just being a prude.

- I feel stupid for being jealous of a computer.

- Men will be men.

An enabling husband may start to pay more attention to his wife, take her out to dinner, call more often, give gifts, or send flowers. For him, these are genuine signs of affection. He truly loves his wife, but fears that he is slowly losing her to an online lover. So he will put up with her cyberflings to save the relationship. In turn, he gives up his own needs and focuses on ways to win her back, as the case of Jason illustrates: "My wife is divorcing me after twelve years because she is in love with a man who lives 2000 miles away. They chat, video, and telephone each other as much as twelve hours a day. She has totally cut me out of her life. She neglects the house, and the only way dishes or laundry get done is if I do them, and I have done it all for five months now. We have three children, ages seven, five, and two. I now take care of all their needs and pick them up after school. She stays up all night until four, five, or even six in the morning and then can't get up to get the kids ready for school. She then sleeps during the morning while our two-year old is left unattended. All she does is scream at me, but talks all lovingly to her online love. I love her. She is everything to me. I've done everything to keep her – tried to be attentive and show her how much I care, but now all she wants is a divorce."

How can you tell if you have become an enabler? Here are some warning signs to determine if you have fallen into an unhealthy pattern. Review this checklist and see how many items you endorse. The more you check, the more likely it is that you have become an enabler. Do you:

_____ Protect your partner from the consequences of his or her behavior?

_____ Deny the obvious?

_____ Make excuses and justifications to others?

_____ Feel responsible for your partner's behavior?

_____ Obsess over your partner's behavior?

_____ Believe that if your partner would only change, all your problems will disappear?

_____ Feel self-doubt and fear?

_____ Feel alone?

_____ Neglect spiritual pursuits, including prayer or mediation?

_____ Experience changes in eating or sleeping patterns?

_____ Become anxious and stressed over your partner's behavior?

_____ Notice your work performance has decreased?

_____ Take over your partner's responsibilities in an effort to keep family life "normal?"

_____ Become over-involved in work or outside activities?

_____ Suffer health problems due to the emotional upheaval?

_____ Withdraw from family and friends?

_____ Engage in sex more frequently to win back your partner?

These reactions are very much like an enabler who tries to compensate for the actions of an addict. While these reactions are normal, they do not help you or your partner. In fact, this type of behavior actually encourages the person to continue the affair instead of taking responsibility for his or her role in the relationship. Therefore, you must end this destructive cycle and decide that you will no longer tolerate the online affair and take corrective action to stop the enabling behavior.

YES - YOUR RELATIONSHIP IS SALVAGABLE

Virtual adultery doesn't have to end in separation, divorce, or even nasty domestic violence battles. Relationships can be saved – but only if you are both committed to making the relationship work. Hope is available for couples who want to rebuild the trust damaged by infidelity online. Communication is an important ingredient in this healing process. To guide you along the journey of rediscovering your partner again in the aftermath of an online affair, I have provided a seven-step plan to help couples work through the road bumps ahead and build a stronger, healthier relationship for the future.

Step 1: Start with Forgiveness

True forgiveness breeds hope, faith, and optimism for a positive future. As one husband explains, "I have begged my wife for forgiveness, although I don't deserve it. I lied to her about everything I did with the computer, but somehow, I must believe that with a lot of help from God, counseling and other resources that we can be strong together once again."

In order to truly be forgiven, the offending partner must ask for forgiveness. If he or she doesn't, it can lead to resentment and block

89

intimacy. As one wife explains, "My husband thought that just because he gave up these online women that everything would be forgotten. But I am still angry. He thinks what he did was no big deal. But it is a big deal. I just can't believe he refuses to see that he did something wrong."

Remember that asking for forgiveness is a symbol that you recognize the hurt you have caused. Without admitting wrongdoing, there is no way for your partner to offer the necessary forgiveness it takes to rebuild the relationship. Also, remember to approach and resolve all problems with complete honesty in order to restore trust and faith in a broken relationship.

Step 2: Say Goodbye to the Past

Like the alcoholic who dumps all the bottles of alcohol down the drain when quitting or the smoker who throws away his last pack of cigarettes, rituals let us say goodbye to the past and symbolizes a fresh start. If you had a cyberlover, end the relationship completely. Often, you can't go back to being "just friends." If you have lied to a cyberlover about your marital status, now is the time to tell the truth and explain why you must say goodbye. Delete old email messages, buddy lists, and/or email addresses. Rituals such as this not only remove reminders of the relationship but also produce closure of that online life. As one wife explains, "Just watching my husband uninstall his ICQ chat software helped me to know he was serious about quitting his addiction to hot sex chat and it put my mind to rest."

Step 3: Use non-blaming "I" statements

Use nonjudgmental language that won't sound critical or blaming. If you say, "You never pay any attention to me because you're always on that damn computer chatting with other women," your partner will perceive it as an attack and act defensively. Instead, use "I" statements that communicate your experience and your feelings. "I feel neglected when you spend long nights on the computer" or ""I feel rejected when you say you don't want to make love with me." If you suspect that your partner is having an online affair but don't have hard evidence, avoid an attack posture that says, "You're screwing around with women all night in those sex rooms and I've had enough of it!" Instead, speak to your real concerns: "I feel hurt that you don't want to talk about our future plans anymore, and I wonder if you've met someone else through the computer."

Stay focused on the present experience. This isn't the occasion to bring up other time-consuming hobbies or obsessions your spouse used to indulge in, which only sounds judgmental. You both should stick with what's happening with the Internet, and avoid trigger words such as "always," "never," "should," or "must." They sound inflexible and invite heated rebuttal. Simple, positive statements will help you each describe how you feel and stay on track.

Step 4: Listen with an open mind

When your partner does respond, stop and listen fully and respectfully. Try to suspend your point of view momentarily and walk in their shoes. Taking this approach does not mean that you lose yourself or agree with their assertions or perspective. Rather, you are demonstrating that you're open to what he or she says and are trying to accept their reality without condemnation. Your receptivity may allow your partner to open up about why they've stumbled into an online affair, and you may be surprised by what you hear. Many spouses explain that they never intentionally sought out a cyberaffair but found the process happening too fast for them to see and understand. Underneath, they may be feeling guilty and truly wish to stop. Or, the online experience may have stirred up their own resentments about the pain over what's been missing for *them* in your marriage. Without suspending your feelings of betrayal or loss of trust, without dropping your need to see your partner make real changes, try to listen to these explanations as openly as possible. Remember also that your facial expression and body language communicate your receptivity or lack of it. Unlike Internet encounters, your communication is multi-dimensional.

Step 5: Consider other communication alternatives

If your attempts at communicating in person fail, don't despair. Try writing your partner a letter. Silly as it may sound to write a letter to the person you live with, you may discover the benefits to a longer forum that allows you to communicate all your thoughts and feelings without interruption from your partner. Reading your letter in a less charged atmosphere may allow him or her to drop his or her defensive posture and respond to you in a more balanced manner. You might even consider communicating by e-mail, which not only offers the same freedom of interruptions as letters but can demonstrate to your partner that you don't view the Internet itself as entirely evil. You both might even share a laugh at the irony of taking this approach, which could open the door to a more productive face-to-face talk.

Step 6: Establish computer ground rules

The computer serves as a sign of infidelity and reminds the couple of past hurts, and it may now trigger feelings of suspicion and jealousy for your partner. In order to increase trust in the relationship, you must establish ground rules for how the computer will be used at home and at work. Simply removing the computer may not be a practical solution, especially if it is needed for work. You both must negotiate a reasonable "computer contract" that specifies exactly how and when the computer will be used, which may include time limits, moving the computer into a public area of the home, or applying monitoring software on the machine.

Step 7: Develop a satisfying sexual relationship

Online affairs can be symptomatic of unmet sexual needs that exist between a couple before the Internet ever entered their lives, but instead of dealing with these issues directly, a partner turned to online sexual stimulation to fulfill his or her needs. In other cases, a couple shared a satisfying sex life prior to the Internet and the online affair creates a new set of difficulties that the couple must deal with. In either case, a couple must make a close examination of their sexual relationship and look for ways it can be improved in order to rebuild intimacy and closeness.

Consider your "pre-Internet" sex life as a couple. Was sex satisfying or did sexual problems exist that you both ignored? This is a time to be completely honest about your feelings. Once you have identified some areas for improvement, you both need to be open-minded to new approaches to lovemaking. While some therapists suggest using cybersex itself to rebuild sexual excitement, I find there is still too much hurt and

92

pain associated with the computer for this to be an effective solution. I suggest finding offline ways to experiment with sex together, whether it's trying a new position, going away for a romantic weekend, or watching erotic movies together, anything that you can both share to rekindle passion and excitement in your sexual relationship.

It must be clear that the final destination is not a return to the "old relationship" but instead create a "new and improved" version. To help make this transition easier, consider couples counseling to improve communication and work through the rough spots. Most importantly, don't be afraid that therapists will laugh at you if you ask for help. There is nothing to be ashamed of, especially as more counselors have come to recognize the devastating effects of cyberaffairs on relationships.

CHAPTER 6

WHAT FAMILIES CAN DO TO HELP A CYBERSEX-ADDICTED LOVED ONE

"They love the best who love with compassion."

Ellen Anne Hill

After a recent lecture in Nebraska, I noticed several women waiting to speak with me gathered in the corner of the room. After most people cleared out and the line dwindled down, I walked over to them. One woman held a copy of my book, *Caught in the Net*, in her hand and said, "My husband has struggled with this addiction for the last six months, and I just didn't know where to turn. I was so relieved to find your book because no one around here knew anything about sex chat rooms or how addictive they are."

Next was an elderly woman who told me about her daughter, a wife and mother of two toddlers, who was having several cyberaffairs. Tears welled up in her eyes as she explained, "Her behavior has just traumatized the whole family. She was the perfect wife and mother until the Internet came into their home. Suddenly, my daughter's entire personality changed. When I tried to talk with her about it, she became angry and defensive. She used to be able to tell me anything, and now she refuses to talk with me."

Yet another woman told me about her sister, and the next one told me about her son. All of them complained that they were frustrated, scared, and confused by the sudden personality changes that took place after cybersex came into their lives.

Time after time, I receive dozens of cries for help from family members of a cybersex-addicted loved one, all in search of validation and guidance with how to confront the problem and deal with the addiction.

ANDREA'S CRY FOR HELP

Andrea is a forty-eight-year-old elementary teacher living in White Plains, New York. She wrote to me about her sister's addiction to cybersex. Her story captures the pain and frustration that concerned family members, children, and friends of the addict often experience.

"My sister, a married mother of three, lost all interest in her children, her husband of twenty-one years, and all other outside activities she had previously been involved in. The change was gradual. At first we were just concerned and irritated, because she was constantly online and no one could reach her. Then she started developing intense online friendships and she has progressed to having what we believe are multiple real sexual relations with men and perhaps women.

We, her daughter and I, have reason to know that these sexual relationships are centered around a bondage theme. In fact, most of the time when she is in a chat room she is engaged in some sort of weird cybersex. We also know that she is engaged in this type of sex with live partners, not just on the Net. We know she plans to visit at least two of these men in the coming months. We are terrified for her and don't know what to do. We fear she is addicted and doesn't care about the cost of her new behavior. She will not stop for anyone.

My niece and I are the only two people in our family who know the extent of the problem. We have tried to protect both my parents and my sister's sons from this because we see no benefit for upsetting them. My sister's husband simply refuses to acknowledge that there is a problem. In fact, he has admitted that sometimes this is a nice change because my sister is off his back. We have not told him the extent of my sister's betrayal. My sister gets calls at all hours from these people. She has changed her dress from that of a normal mom to black lace and tight mini-skirts. She leaves the house at all hours and doesn't return. She goes away for weekends and lies about who she is with. She tells these people she loves them, while she is standing in front of her own family, and then denies a problem.

She is wearing jewelry given to her by these people. Her behavior is just so bizarre, and none of us can believe how enormous the change has been. My sister has always been a terrific, decent, religious, caring person. She was the best mom I knew. She was fun to be with and talk to. Now, I don't believe a word that comes out of her mouth. She lies constantly and doesn't even bother with being consistent. The other thing we thought you should know is that my sister has shown my niece pictures of these people, and they truly look like the dregs of society. It is almost like her self-esteem has lessened with this contact and she is associating with people she never would have before.

I don't live with my sister so her addiction has only caused me anger and worry. Her daughter tells me that her mom stopped cooking dinner, which she did every night for twenty years; she stopped asking her youngest son about school and has not asked for a report card in eighteen months. She does not attend any of his school functions, even though in the past she would never have missed anything. When my niece was home for Christmas her mother, who she was very close to, did not spend a single evening with her. My niece and my sister got into a very harsh argument about these problems and her father sided with her mother, just to make the tensions go away. My parents are very worried, although again, I have not told them everything. My mom is seventy and my dad had by-pass surgery less then a year ago. I don't feel that they need to know as much as I do. Her son in the Navy can never reach home because of her constant usage.

My sister's husband recently began his own online weirdness, sending an advertisement for sexual services. He claims it was a joke. My sister felt the need to call and inform her daughter of this at 7 a.m., obviously in an attempt to say hey, it's not only me. I have failed her in that I have never confronted her on what I see and know. My reasons were that I knew things I wasn't supposed to and I didn't want to upset the rest of the family. I live 800 miles away, so it would be her husband and kids that would take the brunt of my confrontation. My niece and I did not discover that the problem had overflowed into real life and she is meeting these people until about six weeks ago. That is when we searched out and found your book. My niece has confronted her about the danger involved in letting these people have her telephone number and address, but she says they are her friends and she trusts them. Another weird thing that seems to be happening is my sister has told her family enough about the slave master thing that she will openly talk about it, saying it is just a game. We know that it is not, but we think her talking about it is an attempt to take the sting of weirdness away and make it more normal and acceptable.

We are seeking any help we can get. What can we do? Are we too late? We worry that we have become enablers by our passivity. We have considered going to her and confronting her even though we both live out of town. We just aren't sure the best way to proceed and could use advice and insight."

BREAKING THE DENIAL THROUGH FAMILY INTERVENTION

As the case of Andrea illustrates, family members and friends are the first to recognize the loved one's problem. But as the case also shows, family members feel helpless and alone in this knowledge. They don't know where to turn and are not sure how to best confront the cybersex addict. Family members are the first to see the problem, and yet they feel confused, frustrated, angry, hurt, and devastated by the addict's denial and rationalization of the behavior. They fear losing the cybersex-addicted loved one to the disease forever. And they fear being an enabler by doing nothing, yet they aren't sure where to begin to find help for this new, and often, unrecognized disorder.

Like Andrea, a family member struggles with how to talk about the issue, not only with the cybersex-addicted loved one, but even to other family members. How much should they reveal about the extent of the addiction? What will the other family think? Will they laugh or minimize the problem as a passing phase? If they do decide to confront the addict, what do they say? When should they do it? Where should they do it?

Addiction professionals typically suggest conducting what is known as a "family intervention" or a method of confronting the addict into admitting the problem. *Interventionists*, as they are sometimes called, are specialists who assist families in conducting the family intervention. Their services may range from brief consultations to facilitating the actual family intervention. To help family members learn effective ways to approach a cybersex-addicted loved one in denial, I have provided a step-

97

by-step blueprint and intervention guide for family members and friends to follow.

Step 1: Gather everyone together

Family interventions should include everyone concerned for the addict. This may include the immediate family, such as a spouse or partner and age-appropriate children; extended relatives, such as an aunt, uncle, mother, father, sister, brother, or cousin; and trusted friends. Using this book as a guideline, start talking about the issues and begin to carefully examine how this person has changed since becoming involved with cybersex.

In many situations, the spouse or partner is left to feel completely alone because he or she is the only one to witness the early stages of the addictive behavior. If you are a spouse living with the addict and haven't already enlisted the help of your family and friends, now is the time to do so. Don't be afraid that they will laugh. Making a joke out of it is always a possibility, as others may find it hard to believe that someone can become addicted to cybersex. If they do start to minimize the problem, educate them on the severity and full extent of the behavior to help them understand. Show them this book and other research materials associated with Cybersexual Addiction to help them see that this is just as real as alcoholism or drug dependence, and is nothing to laugh at.

Step 2: Develop a list of consequences due to the addiction

Once you have collected everyone together, it is time to reflect on the problems created by the addiction. Each of you should independently generate a list of consequences that you have observed due to the addiction. This process allows you to reflect more deeply about your own hurts caused by the behavior. Keep in mind that this isn't a time to air old issues, but genuinely try to think back to when you first noticed a problem related to the computer. Consider what life was like before the Internet. Generally speaking, Cybersexual Addiction is a quick fall, often less than one year. Given the short development cycle, much less than in comparison to the development cycle for alcoholism or compulsive gambling, it is easier for family and friends to recall what life was like before cybersex.

Ask yourself when you first noticed the shift in behavior. Was it sudden or gradual? Was it little things that slowly weren't getting done around the house, such as the laundry, cooking, or cleaning? Did he become less interested in once cherished events, such as golfing, going to the theater, or playing cards with friends since the Net? Did she spend less time gardening since discovering chat rooms? Your list can range from hobbies the person used to enjoy to specific consequences resulting from excessive online use, such as forgetting to pick up the children from school, losing a big job or promotion at work, failing school, or getting fired. Your list might look like this:

- Having a close, trusting, and loving marriage.
- Stability at the job or being up for a good promotion.
- Going boating on weekends.
- Spending time with the children in the evenings.
- Working on model planes.
- Gardening on the weekends.
- Going on family outings such as to the zoo or sports events.
- Talking on the phone with friends.
- Going out to lunch with friends.
- Keeping in touch and calling relatives.

Your list should be thorough, so try to include as many specific instances as you can possibly think of. When it comes time for the actual family intervention, a clear and comprehensive list will help the person to fully understand your concerns.

One goal of a family intervention is to help the cybersex addict realize the consequences of current behavior and what the future will look like if he or she doesn't stop. To facilitate this awareness of what the addict

99

stands to loose, make a second list of what life will look like if he or she doesn't seek out help. These severe consequences might include:

- Breaking trust and fidelity in the marriage.
- Separation or divorce.
- Being fired at work.
- Money problems.
- Losing one's children in a custody battle.
- Losing one's friends.
- Being arrested (if illegal online activity is present).

Step 3: Share your lists with one another

Next, gather all the family and friends together who will be involved with the intervention and share your lists with one another as a group. Did you all notice any common themes or issues? Did you all notice that his job performance has suffered lately? Have you all noticed that mom seems less interested in the children since meeting her online friends? Have you all noticed that dad no longer spends time doing once cherished activities with the family, such as boating or going to baseballs games, and instead he is always "working" on the computer?

The purpose of this group discussion is not to sit around and "bad mouth" your loved one, but rather to help you each crystallize and prioritize your thoughts and generate a comprehensive picture of the cybersex addict's behavior. This is also a process for family members to reveal secrets and share truths. Andrea explains, "Finally, my niece and I have managed to convey there is a problem to the other members of our family, and they are willing to do whatever it takes - but we have not told them everything. The stuff is too ugly and hurtful. We don't want to tell them, for my sister's sake and for their sake."

Obviously, each situation is a little different, but for the intervention to be effective, it is important that each relative and friend involved understand the extent of the problem. While the truth may be initially painful to hear, it is better to come from the mouth of a loved one at this stage where the information can properly be absorbed and processed, rather than having it revealed during the actual intervention, only to come as a great shock.

The key to this step is to allow family and friends time to openly share feelings and process what living with the addict has been like, in order to gain support and strength from knowing that you are not alone. As one woman explains, "I was so relieved to know that my father also saw my mother's addiction to cyberchats. She even lied to these men about being married to my father. Initially, I felt responsible for my mother's behavior because I taught her how to use the Internet. I carried this guilt with me for months, until we all sat down to talk about the problem. It was so comforting to know that I wasn't alone, and it helped ease my sense of self-blame."

Step 4: Develop a plan for the intervention

It is important to develop a plan for how to execute the family intervention. Time, date, and place should all be considered in this stage. Decide when the best time to have the intervention should be. Should it be in the afternoon or evening? Would it be better after dinner when the person is less likely to be on the Internet? Obviously, the time you designate should maximize the receptiveness of the message, so doing it at the normal time the addict goes online won't be a practical time to choose.

What day is best? Are weekdays less hectic than weekends? Or would weekends be a better time because the person doesn't have to go to work the next morning, leaving him or her time to adjust emotionally to what has been said?

Where should you hold the intervention? Should it be at the addict's home? Or should it be in a neutral place, say at a family member's home or a friend's house? If you decide to have it away from where the addict normally accesses the computer (at his or her home), then you must consider how you will get the addict to arrive at the person's house. What will you tell her? Why does she need to go there? As one family member explains, "We always have Sunday dinner at her daughter-in-law's house. It seemed the only time of the week that she allowed herself to be away from computer." Each step of the family intervention should be discussed ahead of time; however, don't expect every thing to go as planned. Even if you have considered everything, life has a mind of its own, so be prepared for the best laid plans to change.

Step 5: Rehearse the intervention

Returning to Andrea's case, she felt overwhelmed about the prospect of the impending family intervention. "I will admit that my niece and are very uncomfortable about confronting my sister," she explains. "We would love another suggestion. Much of what we know, we learned because we read some e-mail that we shouldn't have. We are in the strange position of being ashamed to have violated her privacy while knowing that someone needs to know what is going on. I am full of nerves thinking about talking to her. What if she gets mad and never talks with us again? I just don't know how I would handle that."

Andrea expresses the typical emotions family members feel towards doing an intervention – dread, worry, apprehension, and fear. What if the addict becomes defensive? What if the addict storms out of the room? What if the addict refuses to listen? These are all possible outcomes that should be considered. What you are about to do isn't easy. No one likes to confront another person, even if it is meant to help.

To help reduce this anxiety, as a family you should rehearse together for the anticipated intervention in a similar fashion actors rehearse for a theatrical play. What you are about to do is very difficult and nothing prepares you for the actual event, but rehearsal will help you each feel more comfortable with the process and minimize apprehension.

Decide who will be the main spokesperson and in what order you will each speak. As you practice together, carefully consider how you will state your concerns. This isn't a situation calling for "tough love" and focusing blame solely on the addict's inappropriate behavior, as this attitude will only produce shame and resistance. Concentrate on using nonjudgmental language that won't sound critical or blaming, and critique each other and refine your statements as necessary. Practice using non-blaming "I" statements that will help your loved one actually hear the message and avoid trigger words such as "always," "never," "should," and "must" that sound like an attack. To enhance the reality of the rehearsal process, enlist a family member to pretend to be the addict. This person should respond in the same way you envision the addict responding, so that you can better anticipate the addict's potential reaction. Finally, try to rehearse as much as possible to help the family prepare to act in a cohesive manner. This type of thoughtful preparation will help you show a united front and send a clear, strong, and confident message that will hopefully save your loved one from self-destruction.

Step 6: Communicate with warmth and caring

Family interventions should be approached in the warm, supportive, and caring manner. In an ideal situation, the intervention should foster an atmosphere designed to:

- Negotiate and express needs.
- Establish and maintain proper boundaries.
- Listen to each other's concerns with respect.
- Be comfortable sharing feelings.
- Encourage honesty and trust.

Despite your best efforts to create a positive atmosphere, your loved one may respond with defensiveness, anger, and resistance. During a recent family intervention one mother stormed out of the house crying, "You just don't understand. I hate you all." Repeated attempts by to her daughters, husband, and mother to encourage her stay and listen failed. In other cases, the person recognizes the addiction, but is extremely embarrassed that the family knows his "dirty little online secret," and feels deeply ashamed during the intervention.

Remember that while you have prepared for the family intervention for days, weeks, or perhaps months, this is the first time your loved one has heard what you have to say. Your loved one may be emotionally unprepared to deal with what is being told to him or her, even if he or she knows it is the truth. Reactions in response to the intervention can come in the following ways:

1. *Denial* – Refuses to accept what is being told.
2. *Withdrawal* – Pulls away from the situation and conflict because of hurt feelings, anger, and resentment.
3. *Shaming* – Feels guilty and ashamed by the family's discovery.
4. *Emotional Cutoff* – Stops all communication and storms out of the room
5. *Threats* – Makes demands, uses ultimatums, or blames family for the problem.
6. *Humor and Sarcasm* – Makes jokes or cutting remarks to shift focus off the conflict.
7. *Manipulation* – Uses guilt and deception to control the family.
8. *Convergence* – Superficially and insincerely agrees with the family to avoid further confrontation.

You should expect a combination of these feelings to emerge and be prepared for the transitional stage that takes place after the intervention. During this transitional phase, your loved one needs time to absorb what has been said and must decide where to go from here. Independent of this person's initial response, there is a period of reflection and discernment to determine the next course of action. This may take days, weeks, or months. Meanwhile, the family is also in transition, as they can no longer pretend that the "white elephant isn't in the room." The Pandora's box is now open, and you must be prepared for how the family will change.

Step 7: Be prepared to treat the family

To maximize recovery for the addict, the family system as a whole must be able to learn new communication skills, establish boundaries, and accept personal commitment for change. However, families falsely believe that the only goal of the intervention is to get the addict into treatment as soon as possible. Many families think that once they have done the intervention, they have finished their part and that the addict must be the one to change.

Family interventions are about much more than getting the addict into treatment. The intervention "event" with the addicted person is only the first step towards recovery. The recovery process must also address the effects of the addiction on the entire family and help the family to recognize and change old patterns of behavior and process what has happened to them as a result of the addict's misuse of the Internet. Families should not scapegoat the addict as the only one with a problem, but they should work together to create a cohesive, open, and positive environment that explores the impact of the family's past history of addictive or high-stress behavior on present-day relationships. With the addict's entire support system involved, the means through which he previously sustained the compulsive behavior are no longer available. Everything changes, and the addict is pulled into that change process. Without this clear-minded insight, the addict may be very successful in a structured treatment program, only to relapse when he returns home because of the unresolved family issues.

Andrea's sister, Margaret, struggled with many life issues prior to the Internet. Margaret was on medication for heart problems, asthma, and a recent hysterectomy. Married twenty-one years, she has three grown children, one in college, one in the navy and one who graduated high school last year. She worked off and on for the last nine or ten years at various jobs, but mainly she was a stay-at-home mom until her children were older and was very devoted to all of them. Her husband Alan worked twelve-hour shifts as a mechanic in a local plant, then came home exhausted, hungry, and tired. He also suffered from a drinking problem. While these events existed in her real life, online she was very popular with her cyberfriends and her virtual world then served as a convenient escape to avoid several unresolved issues in her life:

- Role as a mother changed
- Empty marriage
- Felt isolated and alone by herself each day

- Bored with her daily routine
- Lacked adequate support system of family
- Hadn't cultivated outside hobbies or interests
- Lacked marketable skills to find suitable job
- Suffered from significant health problems over the past year

Margaret felt stuck in her life, but the family didn't realize the emotional pain that she was in. Our family goals included ways to develop a better support system, and to create cohesion within the inter-familial relationships, as well as strategies to improve Margaret's independence.

Margaret enjoyed the attention she received from her cyberlovers because Alan was gone all day at work and slept most of the time he was home. With the children grown up, she felt her purpose in life had changed but without marketable skills, she didn't think she was capable of getting a job. Margaret grew distant from Alan and felt more like a maid than a wife, as her main role in the marriage was doing his cooking, cleaning, and laundry. Alan tried to spend more quality time with her on the weekends. However, the hardest issue to overcome in their marriage was his drinking problem. He refused to admit his own addiction to alcohol, and put the blame on job stress. With the family's help, he was able to see how much his drinking had become out of control and eventually entered Alcoholics Anonymous.

Andrea was able to provide continued support by calling Margaret daily and she even encouraged her to join an aerobics class taught through her church. Over time, Margaret decided to take business courses at the local community college and worked part time in the college library. This not only provided her with a sense of purpose and trained her for future jobs, but now her Internet use focused more on schoolwork and less on chat rooms.

SEEK OUT PROFESSIONAL HELP

While this chapter provides direction, you should seek out the consultation and assistance of a healthcare professional before considering doing an intervention on your own. This type of professional guidance will be instrumental in achieving maximum results with your loved one. With dedication and commitment from the entire family, successful recovery from Cybersexual Addiction is possible.

CHAPTER 7

LOOKING TOWARDS THE FUTURE: FINDING ADDITONAL RESOURCES

"God grant me the serenity to accept the things I cannot change, the courage to change the things I can, and the wisdom to know the difference."

Reinhold Niebuhr

Even with the strong support of loved ones, regaining control of your cybersex habit is a difficult task to complete alone. At some point, it is helpful to at least consider seeking professional guidance to maintain sobriety and avoid relapse. An addiction treatment program, a therapist or counselor who understands Cybersexual Addiction or a good support group can help keep you on track. But how do you find one?

SEEKING PROFESSIONAL HELP

When you begin to seek out a counselor, there are a few things you must first consider. Therapists vary greatly depending upon the level of training, the type of education they have had, and the amount of knowledge that they have about the Internet and cyberaffairs. Specialized and trained professionals in this area are only slowly emerging. If one isn't available in your area, and you are trying to locate the most qualified healthcare professional, consider these five factors when choosing a therapist.

- Find a therapist you feel comfortable with.

- Find a therapist who fully comprehends the nature of your problem.

- Find a therapist you feel you can share a collaborative relationship with.

- Find a therapist who believes that someone can be addicted to the Internet.

- Find a therapist who understands something about the Internet.

In general, entering therapy is a difficult process. And it isn't easy to find a therapist familiar with the Internet, online addiction, and the impact of cyberaffairs. Over time, this will change, but in the meantime, make sure that your therapist is someone willing to listen and learn about the Internet in order to best help you.

Benefits of Group Counseling

Twelve Step Support Groups are an important step in the recovery process. Sharing in the fellowship of those who are also in recovery surrounds the addict with others who have suffered in the same way, helping him to no longer feel unique. Support group participation also helps the addict gain a new sense of pride, improve self-worth, provide encouragement, redefine their core value system, and model new ways of interacting.

Though the Twelve Steps were developed by and for alcoholics, their application has been adapted for those who suffer from other compulsive disorders has led to the formation of other Twelve Step Groups: Gamblers Anonymous, Overeaters Anonymous, Narcotics Anonymous, and Sexual Addicts Anonymous. Using this program, individuals and families who have felt high levels of desperation and pain have been able to turn their lives around. Below I have adapted and applied the Twelve Steps for Cybersexual Addiction:

1. We admitted we were powerless over cybersex – that our lives had become unmanageable.

109

2. Came to believe that the Power greater than ourselves could restore us to sanity.

3. Made a decision to turn our will and our lives over to the care of God, as we understood Him.

4. Made a searching and fearless moral inventory of ourselves.

5. Admitted to God, to ourselves, and to another human being the exact nature of our wrongs.

6. Were entirely ready to have God remove all these defects of character.

7. Humbly asked Him to remove our shortcomings.

8. Made a list of all persons we had harmed, and became willing to make amends to them all.

9. Made direct amends to such people wherever possible, except when to do so would injure them or others.

10. Continued to take personal inventory and when we were wrong promptly admitted it.

11. Sought through prayer and meditation to improve our conscious contact with God, as we understood Him, praying only for knowledge of His will for us and the power to carry that out.

12. Having had a spiritual awakening as the result of these steps, we tried to carry this message to others and to practice these principles in all our affairs.

Accepting that there is a Higher Power is not necessarily about religion, but the Twelve-Step model is a belief system that helps to overcome the temptation when the hard times hit. Relapse is part of recovery, and having a support group will help you to process those moments of relapse and work through the triggers for your Net-binge. Group membership will also help you at the next moment of temptation by providing sponsorship, akin to AA, in order to cope with difficult times during this transition period.

Support group participation also helps you to address conflicting emotions that underlie the addiction. As you struggle with how to co-exist with the Internet and its sexual offerings without indulging, you may also feel angry that you must give up something that makes you feel better about yourself and you may be resentful of others who are trying to take it away from you. In a group of supporters, you can confront these issues and deal with them in a warm, caring atmosphere.

Often, the cybersex addict may try to normalize his behavior: "I'm not as bad as so-in-so. They spend more hours online, they lost their job because of it, they lost their marriage, but I'm okay." In reality, the addict is not okay. A support group will help you to correct this type of self-destructive thinking that only serves to reinforce the addictive behavior.

Sometimes, group participation has the opposite impact, with members becoming competitive with one another about who has the worst battle story. "You did this, but I did that" is the type of mentality shared by some addicts, with each trying to show they are more messed up than the rest. This is a sign of an unhealthy attempt to gain attention from others, and while you may have suffered significantly, you shouldn't compare your situation as better or worse than others. The gift of a support system is to help you understand the uniqueness of your situation. Most importantly, group membership provides an opportunity for you to develop real life relationships through the comfort and understanding of other members. This is especially important as cybersex addicts typically suffer interpersonal difficulties such as introversion and have a limited social network, which is part of the reason they turn to cybersex in the first place. In their world, sexual contact online is a substitute for the lack of real life social connection in their lives. Through the guidance and support of group membership, you won't need to rely on cyberfriends for companionship, and these new relationships will enable you to feel less isolated, so you can focus more clearly on recovery.

Finding a Support Group

While groups that specialize in Cybersexual Addiction are still evolving, you can investigate groups familiar with sexual compulsivity, such as Sexual Recovery Anonymous, Sex Addicts Anonymous, Sexaholics Anonymous, or Sex and Love Addicts Anonymous to build the sense of community currently missing in your life. I have provided additional resources at the end of this chapter to assist you in contacting these organizations. Other possible ways to find a good support group is to contact your local mental health center or drug and alcohol rehabilitation center for referrals. When checking out a possible support group, it is important to ask yourself:

- Do you feel comfortable in that group's environment?
- Do members appear welcoming to you and your problems with the Internet?
- Do you believe that members will understand your goals and validate your efforts to reach them?

In asking the right questions when evaluating a group, you may even be led to others who are wrestling with the same problems. You may find yourself part of a newly forming group just for cybersex addicts! Many people are frustrated when they can't find a support group that specializes in Internet/Cybersexual Addiction recovery, so they get interested in being pioneers by starting their own support group. I strongly recommend talking with a local mental health counselor to find out about community and state-based issues related to running a support group in your area, as each community and state abides by different rules and policies.

Secondly, I would suggest reviewing the information at the National Mental Health Consumers' Self-Help Clearinghouse. The web address is http://www.mhselfhelp.org. They provide services that will help you develop a local support group. The National Clearinghouse's technical assistance is designed to provide information for members of mental health consumer groups who wish to improve their facilitation skills. Clearinghouse staff can address issues such as introducing discussion topics, speakers and presentations, improving your communication skills, and developing long-term goals. When considering starting your own support group, they outline three basic guidelines:

1. **Find out what groups exist in your area** - These groups can provide proven workable models for the development of your own group.

2. **Enlist the help of others** - Seek out individuals who share your interests to help get the group going. These original members will serve as a planning committee.

3. **Develop a project plan** - Hold an organizational meeting to address the following questions: What is the purpose of the group? Who are we trying to reach? How will we recruit participants? How will we work with other available services? Where will we meet?

National Mental Health Consumers' Self-Help Clearinghouse Plan for First Meeting:

- Write an agenda.

- Decide on roles.

- Plan to allow time to discuss your project plan as well as receive input from new members.

- Plan to have refreshments and some time for socialization.

- Discuss what each member will bring to the meeting.

- Be sure that your core group of organizers has discussed and reached a consensus on the general purpose, goals, and membership of the group.

- Meet with the planning group at least a half-hour before the meeting is scheduled to take place to go over these ideas.

The First Meeting: An Overview

One or several members of the planning group should meet and greet newcomers at the door. Begin by stating the group's possible purposes and goals. Explain that the group is designed to meet the needs of its members so their input will determine the goals as well. Brainstorm with the group by having the members describe what they hope to gain from the group. Use a black board, or easel to post these goals. Attempt to narrow down these goals into a smaller list that everyone can agree on. At future meetings, develop an "action plan" to work on achieving these goals. Encourage new members to share, but don't pressure them. Try to stick to your original agenda, but be flexible and allow members to speak freely. Let new group members know that they are welcome in the planning process. Discuss the agenda for the next meeting. Divide tasks, such as bringing in refreshments, among willing members.

Encourage group participation as a means to meet the goals of the group and establish ground rules for communication. Before the structured portion of the meeting is over, pass around a contact sheet to obtain names and numbers of new group members and make sure they have the name and number of a contact person. Establish when and where your group will meet in the future. Finally, thank everyone for coming and invite everyone to stay and enjoy some refreshments.

Keep in mind that the first meeting is an opportunity to introduce group members and get a sense of group expectations. It may take one or two more meetings similar to this one to increase group membership and participation. When the group is ready, you can begin to discuss more specific organizational issues such as purpose, meeting format, roles, and phone networks.

IS DETOX NEEDED?

In a growing number of cases, the need to have cybersex may be so powerful that treatment requires you to go through a *detox* program, in the same manner an alcoholic goes through a detox program to dry out. While the concept of detox as part of the recovery from alcoholism is well understood, it is still a relatively new intervention applied to Cybersexual Addiction, but one that must be explored in severe cases where abstinence from online sexual behavior is not possible. One software developer had to go two years without any Internet access in order to deal with his addiction to online pornography. In another case, a working mother of two had to admit herself into a twenty-eight-day inpatient drug and alcohol rehabilitation center to curb her addiction to erotic chat rooms. You should consult with the proper medical and psychiatric professionals before considering a detox program. Don't feel weak-willed, strange, or even silly in discussing your situation with a professional to assess the need for detox from a computer. For many, it is the only alternative to building a healthier life.

INCREASED AWARENESS

Although going online for sexual pursuits does not necessarily cause problems or inevitably lead to inappropriate sexual acting out, increased awareness seems the best way to help users understand the long-term effects of this type of addictive behavior. On way to increase awareness is directly through computer training classes. As more adults seek out professional training to build computer skills, it is essential that we focus on ways to help in prevention of Cybersexual Addiction at this early stage of learning. Training classes for adult computer users should extend beyond just how to use the Internet to include information on how not to *abuse* the Internet. To encourage responsible use, classes should outline indicators for users to assess whether a user's behavior might make him vulnerable, criteria for when to seek therapy, and information on how to locate networks of qualified providers and moderated chats offered by church groups, mental health associations, and treatment centers. Also, to aid in prevention and better prepare Internet consumers for the possible risks of cybersex use, public service announcements could be launched to warn individuals and families about the potential dangers of online sexual experimentation.

A WORD TO PARENTS

Finally, a note to parents as statistics show that computer-enabled sex increasingly impacts children and adolescents. In our homes, children are the primary reason behind household decisions to purchase a computer and gain Internet access. And the number of children going online is rising every year. The Grunwald Associates, a California marketing firm, found that there are now twenty million two-to-seventeen-year olds on the Web, up from eight million since 1997. By the year 2005, the number of children online is expected to increase by another seventy percent, the survey projected.[1] However, the revitalization of the child porn industry places children at greater risk to be abducted, as pornographers need them to manufacture new photographs and movies.

Sexual offenses against children constitute a significant proportion of all reported criminal online sex acts. A study conducted by the Crimes Against Children Research Center at the University of New Hampshire found the following statistics related to child online victimization:

1 in 4 children who've gone online have been solicited

1 in 5 has been sent provocative pictures thru web contact

725,000 have been asked to meet for sexual purposes[2]

Cyberspace isn't policed the way real life hangouts are and to complicate matters, teen online dating and sexual experimentation is on the rise, making it easier for online victimization to occur. Unlike giggling about sex at a slumber party with her friends, a young girl is more likely to first learn about sex in a chat room. Instead of buying a Playboy, a young boy is more likely to download pornography directly off the Internet. As more and more children venture online, more and more parents are nervous about the implications created by computer sex. As one panic-stricken mother explains, "I was suspicious and used a pair of binoculars through an open window to spy on my fifteen-year-old daughter, only to discover she was having cybersex with men in their thirties and forties." When the mother confronted her daughter, she replied, "Chill out, mom, everyone is doing it."

In another case, a teenaged-girl from Pennsylvania dated a boy from Germany. Instead of going out to a movie or for ice cream, they met online every weekend for "chat dates." Her parents feared, and rightfully so, whether this virtual boyfriend was in reality a pedophile in disguise. But they had no way of verifying his identity as he lived in another country and they were forced to trust "words on a screen" in the hopes that their daughter would be safe. In other cases, parents simply don't understand how easy it is for a predator to sexually assault a child online. Other times, parents utilize filtering software to protect their children when online; however, they underestimate how easy it is for a computer-literate adolescent to dismantle this software. In fact, several web sites are available that show teenagers how to get around it.

To help parents learn instructive ways to promote safe Internet use and aid in the prevention of future problems, the Center for OnLine Addiction has developed an educational video for parents entitled, "*Net Savvy Parenting: A Guide to Raising Healthy and Safe E-Children.*" The video explains the hazards of computer sex for children and describes how with the Internet, unlike television, government regulators do not censor inappropriate and unsuitable material for children online. As many parents are unfamiliar with the Internet, the video includes a live chat room demonstration to show parents firsthand the ins and outs of cyberspace and shows parents how to determine appropriate time limits surrounding online usage for children and addresses emergent issues such as teen online dating. Finally, the video teaches parents how to safeguard their children when online through the use of various types of parental control software such as *NetNanny*, *CyberPatrol*, and *SurfWatch* and explains family-friendly Internet Service Providers, such as *Mayberry USA*, that screen out unsuitable content for children from their server. For more details or to order a copy, visit our web site at www.ebehavior.com.

It takes a concerted and collective effort to create a safe place for children in cyberspace. To achieve that goal, hopefully Internet service providers (ISPs) and the online adult entertainment industry themselves can play a major role in aiding in the prevention of future problems. These groups can provide close supervision of inappropriate online conduct, especially as related to potential crimes against children. Already, we have seen progress as the adult entertainment industry has been very responsive to these concerns and incorporated a number of changes, such as offering Web site monitors and requiring that a credit card be used at sites so that minors are denied access.

ABOUT THE AUTHOR

Dr. Kimberly Young is an internationally known expert on Internet addiction and online relationships. She is a licensed psychologist and the Executive Director of the Center for Online Addiction. Dr. Young has written numerous papers and articles on the topic, and she is author of *Caught in the Net,* the first book to address Internet addiction recovery, already translated in four languages. She is on faculty at the University of Pittsburgh at Bradford and St. Bonaventure University, and has testified regarding her pioneer research for both civil and criminal legal cases, and most recently, for the Child Online Protection Act Congressional Committee. Her work has been featured in hundreds of newsprint publications worldwide including major articles in The Wall Street Journal, USAToday, The New York Times, Newsweek, and Time and she is a frequent commentator for numerous radio and television programs including *NPR, the BBC, CNBC News, Fox News, Good Morning America*, and *ABC's World News Tonight.* Currently, she travels nationally as a workshop leader on how technology impacts human behavior, including seminars for the National Council on Sexual Addiction and Compulsivity, the American Psychological Association, the European Union on Health and Medicine, and the first International Congress on Internet Addiction held in Zurich, Switzerland.

ABOUT THE CENTER FOR ONLINE ADDICTION

Founded in 1995, the Center for Online Addiction is the first independent healthcare clinic and training institute to specialize in cyber-related psychological issues such as cybersexual addiction, infidelity online, information overload, and compulsive day trading. The Center conducts diagnostic and forensic evaluations and provides outpatient clinical services to individuals and families. The Center is internationally recognized as a leader in the field and conducts training seminars worldwide for healthcare organizations, law enforcement agencies, and corporations.

The company's Web site at Netaddiction.com provides both dynamic and static content related to the psychology of cyberspace to increase public awareness on the implications of Internet addiction and related online mental health concerns. The site also features a comprehensive resource center complete with message boards, research articles, referral links to other mental health sites, self-evaluation tests, chat support, and an electronic newsletter.

To better serve the growing demand for treatment, the Center for Online Addiction launched the first **Virtual Clinic** in 1997 that specializes in confidential help for cyber-related problems. The Virtual Clinic offers individual electronic or telephone sessions designed to provide crisis management, directions in family interventions, and personal counseling. For more information, please visit www.netaddiction.com or call 814-362-7045 or email info@netaddiction.com.

Dr. Kimberly S. Young

ADDITIONAL RESOURCES

Recovery and Referrals:

Center for Internet Studies
www.virtual-addiction.com

Cyberwidows Help
www.cyberwidows.com

Computer Addiction Services
McLean Hospital
www.computeraddiction.com

Sierra Tucson
www.sierratucson.com

Sexual Recovery Institute
www.sexualrecovery.com

International Society of Mental Health Online
www.ismho.org

National Council on Sexual Addiction and Compulsivity
1090 S. Northcase Parkway, Suite 200 South
Marietta, GA 30067

Dr. Kimberly S. Young

(770) 989-9754

www.ncsac.org

National Mental Health Consumers' Self-Help Clearinghouse.

http://www.mhselfhelp.org

Twelve Step Recovery Resources

Adults Anonymous Molested as Children

AAMAC World Services Organization

P.O. Box 662

Apple Valley, CA 92307

COSA (Partners)

9337-B Katy Freeway, Suite 142

Houston, TX 77024

(612) 537-6904

Co-Sex and Love Addicts Anonymous (COSA)

P.O. Box 14537

Minneapolis, MN 55414

(612) 537-6904

Incest Survivors Anonymous (ISA)

P.O. Box 17245

Long Beach, CA 90807-7245

(562) 428-5599

Recovering Couples Anonymous (RCA)
P.O. Box 11872
St. Louis, MO 63105
(314) 830-2600

Sexual Recovery Anonymous (SRA)
P.O. Box 73
Planetarium Station
New York, NY 10024
(212) 340-4650

Sex Addicts Anonymous (SAA)
P.O. Box 70949
Houston, TX 77270
(713) 869-4902

S-Anon (Partners)
P.O. Box 111242
Nashville, TN 37222
(615) 833-3152

Sexaholics Anonymous (SA)
P.O. Box 111910
Nashville, TN 37222-1910
(615) 331-6230

Sexual Compulsives Anonymous (SCA)
West Coast:
    P.O. Box 4470
    170 Sunset Blvd, #520
    Lost Angeles, CA 90027
    (310) 859-5585

East Coast:
    P.O. Box 1585
    Old Chelsea Station
    New York, NY 10011
    (212) 439-1123

Sex and Love Addicts Anonymous (SLAA)
The Augustine Fellowship
P.O. Box 650010
West Newton, MA 02165
(617) 332-1845

S-Anon Family Groups
P.O. Box 5117
Sherman Oaks, CA 91413
(818) 990-6910

Reading Suggestions:

Addictive Thinking: Understanding Self-Deception
By Abraham Twerski, MD
Harper Collins, 1990

Online Seductions: Falling in Love With Strangers on the Internet
By Esther Gwinnell
Kodansha International, 1998

Caught in the Net: How to Recognize the Signs of Internet Addiction and Winning Strategy for Recovery
By Dr. Kimberly Young
John Wiley and Sons, 1998

The Psychology of the Internet
By Patricia M. Wallace
Cambridge University Press, 1999

Hidden Dangers of the Internet: Using It Without Abusing It
By Gregory L. Jantz, Ann McMurray (Contributor)
Harold Shaw Pub, 1998

Virtual Addiction: Help for Netheads, Cyberfreaks, and Those Who Love Them
By Dr. David Greenfield
New Harbinger Press, 1999

Dr. Kimberly S. Young

Hazelden Educational Materials:

Hazelden Educational Materials
1-800-328-9000

Codependent No More
By Melody Beattie

Out of the Shadows: Understanding Sexual Addiction
By Patrick Carnes, Ph.D.

Each Day a New Beginning: Daily Meditations for Women

Touchstones: Daily Meditations for Men

Days of Healing, Days of Joy
By Larnie Larsen & Carol Larsen Hegarty

NOTES

Chapter 1:

[1] Campbell, R. "Mother addicted to Internet loses custody of her kids." *The Orlando Sentinel*. October 22, 1996, pp. 1-2.

Chapter 3:

[1] Young, K.S. (2000) Cybersexual Addiction Survey Results.

http://www.netaddiction.com/cybersexual_addiction.htm

[2] Schneider, J. P. (2000). Effects of Cybersexual Addiction on the Family: Results of a Survey. *Sexual Addiction and Compulsivity*, vol. 7, 31-58.

[3] Cooper, A., Delmonico, D., & Burg, R. (2000). Cybersex users, abusers, and compulsives: New findings and implications. *Sexual Addiction & Compulsivity*, vol. 7, 5-29.

[4] McLaughlin, J.F. (2000). *Technophilia: A Modern Day Paraphilia*.

http://www.ci.keene.nh.us/police/technophilia.html

[5] United States of America versus Kenneth McBroom. No. 96-5719. August 28,1997; United States of America versus Kenneth McBroom. No. 95-502. January 13,1998.

[6] Carnes, P. (1992). *Out of the Shadows.* Center City, Minnesota: Hazelden.

Chapter 5:

[1] Pullella, P. (2000) Internet Adultery a Sin, Catholic Magazine Says. Reuters News Service, Source: amiglia Christiana (Christian Family), June, 2000 Edition.

[2] Young, K, Cooper, A., Griffin-Shelley, E., Buchanan, J, & O'Mara, J. (2000) Cybersex and Infidelity Online: Implications for evaluation and treatment. *Sexual Addiction and Compulsivity.* 7(1), 59-74.

[3] Cooper, A., Scherer, C., Boies, S. C., & Gordon, B. (1999). Sexuality on the internet: From sexual exploration to pathological expression. *Professional Psychology*: Research and Practice, 30(2), 154-164.

[4] Young, K.S. (1998). *Caught in the Net.* New York: John Wiley and Sons.

[5] Young, K S. (1998) Internet Addiction: The emergence of a new clinical disorder. *CyberPsychology and behavior*, 1 (3), 237 – 244.

[6] Quittner, John. "Divorce Internet Style," *Time*, April 14, 1997, p. 72.

Chapter 7:

[1] CBS News Healthwatch at
http://cbsnews.cbs.com/now/story/0,1597,197288-412,00.shtml

[2] UNH Study Finds Many Youth Exposed to Sexual Solicitation, Pornography and Harassment on Internet, University of New Hampshire Crimes Against Children Research Center, June 8, 2000.

Printed in the United States
21675LVS00005B/310-525